SOME REVOLUTIONARY PREMISES OF THE AUTHOR

1. NO ONE is *totally* satisfied with her house, ever. Not even your mother-in-law.
   (Is anyone ever totally satisfied with her life?)

2. You will never, NEVER, be totally satisfied with your house and finished with everything you want to do. Happiness is a reasonable compromise with your superego.

3. The problems you have in housekeeping are inevitable and reflect your personality as clearly as the way you dress.

4. The fault lies neither in your stars, nor in your cleaning woman, nor in your detergent, but in yourself.

But, help is on the way! You *can* make things better. All you need is a little willpower and this book, this helpful, cheerful, easy-to-read and above all, *understanding* book. You are not alone.

The incomparable 20th century classic, a chronicle of family life and enduring love familiar to millions of readers and viewers

THE FORSYTE SAGA
by
John Galsworthy

For the first time as popular-priced paperbacks, from Ballantine Books

A Man of Property
In Chancery
To Let

The White Monkey
Silver Spoon
Swan Song

Maid in Waiting
Flowering Wilderness
One More River

NOBODY SAID YOU HAD TO EAT OFF THE FLOOR...

The Psychiatrist's Wife's Guide to Housekeeping

Carol G. Eisen

BALLANTINE BOOKS • NEW YORK
An Intext Publisher

BALLANTINE BOOKS, INC.
101 Fifth Avenue, New York, N.Y. 10003

Dedication

To my husband, without whom this book would
have to have been subtitled *Somebody Else's
Guide to Housekeeping,* and without
whose forbearance it might well
have been subtitled *The
Psychiatrist's Ex-Wife's
Guide to House-
keeping.*

Contents

Acknowledgments

First of all, there was Senator Eugene J. McCarthy, who had a whole lot to do with it because I wrote a book about him that sold so few copies that Victor Navasky, Marvin Kitman, Richard Lingeman, and Susan Edmiston, who had conned me into writing *that* book, got to feeling all guilty and gave me the idea for this book.

Instrumental were my friends, especially Harriet Bergmann and Jill Spelman, whose incessant calls asking, "Well, did you get it done yet?" enabled me to get it done in only three times what I'd originally allowed. Nancy Alloggiamento read some of it early on and laughed in the right place, providing the encouragement to go on with it. The fact that the part she laughed at was subsequently cut out must mean something, although I'm not exactly sure what. My editor, Eleanor Rawson, who was uniquely able to see the trees when I was mired in the deepest part of the forest, probably knows.

I would like to acknowledge my mother-in-law, who not only gave me the answers to crucial questions like how does one actually wax a floor, but took care of my children in moments of greatest need. My thanks also go to Smith, Kline, and French, the makers of Dexedrine, which allowed me to use every minute in those moments of greatest need. And to God, for the very nice sunrises he thoughtfully provided.

I suppose I should acknowledge Sigmund Freud as

well as the entire membership of the American Psycho-analytic Association, which will probably blacklist this book.

I have used a whole lot of stupid housekeeping books in the course of writing this one, but I didn't plagiarize anything and I threw them all out in a fit of pique a few days ago.

Then there are my children, Michael and Jane, about whom you will read, who will probably grow up with a fear of typewriters. They were, all things considered, pretty good about it.

C. E.

New York, New York

September, 1970

A Preface and Also a Fable

Preface

Contrary to popular belief, it is absolutely untrue that psychiatrists can read minds. Only analysts can do that. But psychiatrists, by the very nature of their profession, do spend a lot of time examining motives—the things that make us do the things we do, good or bad. And wives, by the very nature of their profession, spend a lot of time listening to their husbands talk about their jobs.

So it seems inevitable that, as a psychiatrist's wife, I would spend a lot of time thinking about motives for having a sloppy house (when I should have been cleaning the bathtub instead) and that, as a woman, I would wonder why most of the women I know have similar problems—although each botches up things in her own inimitable style.

This book was written as a result of these musings to try to help the very many of us who have such a terrible time keeping our houses together. Maybe if we can understand the motives and patterns of our behavior, we can find it a little easier to succeed at the most damnable and demanding job ever devised—runing a house.

As I sit here surveying the carnage in the kitchen, my one hope is that this book will make me rich enough so that next year I can afford both an analyst and a full-time maid.

The Four Little Pigs

Once upon a time there were three little pigs. Only they were girl pigs and actually there were four of them. But to get on with it:

Once upon a time there were four little girl pigs who lived with their husbands and piglets in four little houses. One day, the first little pig was sitting reading the list of ship arrivals and departures in her newspaper when she heard a knock at the door. Opening it, she beheld an elderly wolf carrying an attaché case.

"Worry not, little pig," said the wolf, noting her dismay. "I have not come to eat you up, being on a low cholesterol diet because of my age. Rather, I am employed by Herbert, the Good Housekeeper Seal who is seeking to find the perfect homemaker and award her one million dollars and an all-expense-paid trip to Paris."

"Oh my," said the first little pig whose name was Marjorie, "my house is such a mess today. You see, I feel that being a perfect homemaker lies not so much in whether the kitchen floor is clean, but rather in my keeping up my interest in what is going on in the world and not wasting my College Education."

The wolf went next to the house of the second little pig, whose name was Daphne. He was impressed by her pulchritude, even for a pig, and for a time was tempted to go off his diet. Daphne invited him in for a cup of coffee, quickly washing off two cups from the pile in the sink. She told the wolf all about herself and how she felt that keeping a house clean was not quite as important as being A Woman. And anyway, what did it all matter?

At the next house the wolf stood ringing the bell for a long time. Finally, a little pig wearing an artist's smock came to the door.

"Come in, come in," said Topsy Pig. "Let me show you my studio first." She led the wolf to a bright sunny room which would have been worthy of a Leonardo and showed him several interesting canvases. Intrigued, the wolf asked if he might see the rest of the house. Topsy tripped gaily through the rooms, showing him an ashtray she had made, a painting here, an etching there. But the wolf's asthma started acting up from the dust, and he had to leave. "I would keep my house clean, if I only knew how," shouted the pig after him.

When he walked up the path to Betty's house, the wolf was immediately impressed by the neat floral border and the gaily striped air-conditioner covers. A rather harassed pig came to the door and, after he convinced her he wasn't selling anything, admitted him. The house was impeccable and the wolf thought for a minute he had a winner. Complimenting Betty on her home, he was surprised to hear her begin to apologize for the state of disorder—which was totally invisible to him. Before he could ask any more questions, Betty dropped off suddenly to sleep in a comfortable chair. As he left, the wolf noted that she had been sifting the pebbles out of the dirt in the yard.

That night the four little pigs cried themselves to sleep. They cried because they weren't going to get a million dollars. And they cried because they weren't going to Paris. But mostly they cried because they knew they were lousy homemakers and they didn't see any way to change.

Herbert the Good Housekeeper Seal still has his million dollars, and the wolf, having failed in his search for the perfect homemaker, is now out looking for an honest TV repairman.

I

Why You'll Never Get It All Done

Maybe you shouldn't be reading this book right now.

Oh, of course you bought it for the right reasons. Just like you bought the other fifteen books that tell you how to wax your kitchen floor in half the time. Nonsense! If you'd waxed it yesterday, you wouldn't have to worry about it today. Or perhaps you think that when you've finished reading the book you'll do a much better job of pleasing your family. Don't be silly. If you *really* want to please them, there's still time enough before dinner to go into the kitchen and make something more interesting than meatloaf. That's not it either? Perhaps you think this book will make you more economical. Well, really. How many steaks could you have bought with the money you've spent on cookbooks and things that tell you how to keep house?

If you've read this far, it's obvious that you think that something is wrong with your housekeeping.

But why? Unless you're awfully far gone, it's doubtful that anyone entering your house will contract typhoid or impetigo. Your family is not suffering from malnutrition. And you're probably even a bit proud of your home at times.

But you're bothered with the idea that somehow, somewhere, sometimes things could be better. So you pick up this book with the rather desperate hope that, unlike the other books you've read, this will make that difference.

It might.

But only if you can accept some revolutionary premises:

1. NO ONE is *totally* satisfied with her house, ever. Not even your mother-in-law. (Is anyone ever totally satisfied with her life?)
2. You will never, NEVER, be totally satisfied with your house and finished with everything you want to do. Happiness is a reasonable compromise with your superego.
3. The problems you have in housekeeping are inevitable and reflect your personality as clearly as the way you dress.
4. The fault lies neither in your stars, nor in your cleaning woman, nor in your detergent, but in yourself.

With this in mind, and amazingly small effort, things *can* get better.

If you've ever worked as a secretary you probably remember days when your boss kept shoving dictation at you, the telephone never stopped ringing, and, in the middle of everything, your coffee container fell into your typewriter. But the minute you slammed the door of the office shut, you were home free and finished.

Now imagine that it's 7:30 and your guests are expected for dinner at 8:00. By some miracle, everything is done. The maid came today and there isn't a visible speck of dust anywhere. The table is set with freshly polished silver and with crystal goblets that reflect the sparkle of the chandelier against your clean window. Sinking slowly into the nearest chair, you open the morning newspaper for the first time that day. Immediately an ad for a silver vase reminds you that there's still time to cut some fresh flowers from the garden and arrange them charmingly as a centerpiece.

Or maybe it occurs to you that someone might open the medicine chest in the bathroom which reminds you that you have to clear out the expired medicine one of these days before someone gets poisoned. And come to think of poison, wouldn't the green beans look better with some slivered almonds on top? So, depending on the kind of person you are, you will either dash off to the garden and be sponging dirt off your dress when the guests come, or you will do nothing and feel guilty about it, or you will sink into the cushions a little deeper and try to convince yourself that your friends don't like almonds that much anyway.

So you see (and you might try writing this rule five hundred times in the dust on top of your kitchen cabinets)

YOU WILL NEVER GET IT ALL DONE.

And don't think for one minute that your friend up the street who has a neat medicine chest and flowers on the table and almonds on the stringbeans is any different. *She's* probably wondering if she should change the lettering on the placecards from gothic to roman.

There is one very good reason and one very interesting reason why you will never be satisfied that your work is fully done: the very nature of housekeeping is so open-ended that as soon as one job is completed, two others spring up in its place. You'll never get it all done because IT'S INFINITE. And being infinite, unstructured, and undefined, it provides a remarkably fertile area for you to express your own hangups.

Four Dirty Stories
or, Case Histories of Some Housekeeping Failures

In the town of Middletouppermiddleville live four young women. They have virtually identical houses, their husbands make virtually identical salaries, and, curiously enough, none of them has either a maid, a child, or a job. Although their identically loving and solicitous husbands are not too hard on them, each— with one interesting exception—has been gently asked why the house is such a mess.

Marjorie

Mind Over What Matters
If you look carefully beneath the pile of periodicals Marjorie subscribes to, you can sometimes find her. She's not an unattractive girl, but she spends so little time on her appearance that she's beginning to look, in her plaid skirt and round-collar blouse, like a superannuated college sophomore. Marjorie is fun to talk to, but if you wander off the subject she's on, she's apt to look vacant and start talking about starving children. At parties, she's either surrounded by people waving posters supporting her cause or alone in a corner haranguing some hapless visiting cousin of the hostess.

Since she left college, Marjorie has not been idle. She's taken a raft of night school courses ranging from international politics to "The Meaning of Peanut Butter in the Civil Rights Struggle." When Marjorie gets finished reading the newspaper she can tell you when the *Queen Elizabeth* is sailing for Southampton and whether soybean futures are up or down. As soon as she can she's going back to school for her master's degree in Comparative Ambiguities, but for now she has no intention of letting her education go to waste. Her house is almost uniformly dirty and messy.

In the morning, after Marjorie finishes reading her paper, knowing her husband's feeling about breakfast dishes on the table at dinner time, she shoves them in the dishwasher. She doesn't scrape them. On this morning, she decides to weed out the magazines that have been accumulating for three months, but as she starts discarding them, an article on Government Nationalization of the Mafia catches her eye and before she knows it it's time to go off to protest the new zoning laws. She gets home in time to make dinner, but having had no time to go marketing she pulls down a can of tomato sauce and some spaghetti. At dinner, Marjorie is such a brilliant conversationalist that her husband hardly notices that there's nothing but water to drink. "Oh dear," says Marjorie, as she explains to her husband why a draft lottery is better than a volunteer army, "I did mean to get some wine and go marketing."

There's no question in Marjorie's mind that someone as competent as she could have a cleaner house if she really were willing to spend the time. She genuinely *would* like to be able to do a better job of housekeeping. But, as she told her husband, her friends, and anyone else who would listen to her, it's more important to be a companion to your husband and to keep up with what's happening in the World. After all, expecting someone with her brains to spend all her time doing housework is just not fair. Not only is housekeeping scary, but secretly she's afraid her mind will decay while she does it.

Who knows what fantasies and fears lurk in the psyche of Marjorie that make it virtually impossible for her to wash the kitchen floor—when she knows she ought to—and that must be laid to rest with a compulsive job like rearranging her underwear accord-

ing to manufacturer. Marjorie, like all the rest of us,
may need to be a slob.

Daphne

Moonlight and Roaches

In high school it was Daphne who always had the
most dates. Her personality was so charming that she
even had a lot of girl friends who weren't particularly
jealous about how popular she was with boys. Perhaps
it was her looks, although examined closely she's not
all that pretty. She just seems to be able to make the
most of herself, to choose clothes that are flattering
and to bring off color combinations that would look
ridiculous on anybody else. Although her parents
wanted her to go to college, Daphne married her high
school sweetheart, the captain of the football team.

Daphne is the sort of person who always gets the
best steak from the butcher, and when she orders fruit
from the store, it's exactly ripe. Men seem to want to
do things for her. This is not to say, and you should
not for a minute think of such a terrible thing, that
Daphne is to be confused with her friend Deirdre who
gets marvelous cuts from the butcher by sleeping with
him. Daphne uses her sex appeal, it's true, but with
her it's subliminal and second nature. She sees life in
terms of the effect people have on her and she on them
—and she's intensely distressed if someone doesn't
like her, or if she thinks that someone might not like
her. Her antennae are always quivering—it would be
nice if she could turn them off or down from time to
time.

Daphne is the center of the group at almost any
party, though if you listen to her talk you may find
her opinions and comments somewhat superficial. But
Daphne's no dope. And she *sounds* pretty original—

provided you don't read the same magazines she does.

On the whole, Daphne's house is pretty messy; she doesn't pay very much more attention to it than Marjorie does. But on days she feels good, she almost always takes the time to make a good dinner and at least run the vacuum over the rug. On days Daphne feels bad, or when she has one of her headaches (she's sure they're migraines), she usually cajoles her husband into taking her out to dinner. On those days the place is such a mess that he doesn't mind getting out himself. One of the reasons Daphne's considering doing more about keeping her house up is that she's sure people disapprove of her for being such a slob.

Daphne knows how to be female, an enviable and estimable quality, but that's not quite the same as being a homemaker. Charm, conversation, and sex appeal are so natural to her and have worked so well for her in the past that she can't understand why they don't make her house cleaner. Her concern for herself (in many ways useful) may make it difficult for her to appreciate fully that others exist and need to be actively cared for, too.

To get into the habit of being a better housekeeper will probably be difficult and extremely trying at first, if you're something like Daphne. You'll have to allot a specific period of time to doing something that is repugnant to you and foreign to your personality. But it should be possible to integrate housekeeping into the rest of your life.

It may help you to realize that you'll be even more charming to others if you do.

Topsy

My Mother Didn't Bring Me Up to Be a Maid

From her earliest fingerpaintings at the age of eighteen months Topsy showed promise. Her parents were pleased and never made a fuss when she went off after dinner to sketch while her older sisters helped with the dishes. Born rather late in her parents' life, she remained at home until just before her marriage. People always liked her rather charming naiveté about practical matters, and she played the role of a talented ingenue for all it was worth. She still does. She also plays up her vague resemblance to Mia Farrow. Not that she's necessarily aware of all this all the time.

After high school, Topsy went to art school and now she paints at home. The coat closet has been turned into storage space for her not uninteresting canvases, and a corner of the bedroom is devoted to her painting paraphernalia. Sometimes Topsy genuinely enjoys keeping house. She's especially fond of making cute centerpieces for the dinner parties she throws for her friends, who adore her, since she is always available to look after their children. Her friends usually don't mind the warmed-over lasagna served three hours after their arrival.

Topsy's husband, who is ten years older than she is, has suggested more than once that they have his business associates over for dinner sometime, but she thinks it's rather unreasonable for him to suggest that she expend the immense effort to do something suitable. Topsy likes her husband to go with her when she buys her clothes (if her mother isn't available), and her house has the somewhat overdone look of the town's best decorator. Since Topsy housekeeps in spurts, dirt is more of a problem than clutter, but she did notice the other day that she'd bought celery seed for the fifth time in as many weeks because she can't find the rest of it.

Quite simply, Topsy hasn't grown up yet. She has been coddled and babied most of her life, and it's a nice way to feel. She was taught that she could make magic, and, like Daphne, she's surprised that she can't transform her house with a wave of her wand. She is a child playing house with grown-up toys, and Mommy isn't there to clean up after her any more.

If you're a Topsy, you may feel confused and anxious about your house, particularly if you're criticized. It's harder for you to keep a house clean than it is for almost anyone else because you don't know how and to learn may mean giving up the glorious illusion that you're still really a child. You need to be taken gently by the hand and taught the mechanics of housekeeping, learning exactly what to do in the time you feel you can spare.

Betty

I Always Wash My Hands Before I Wash My Hands

Everyone knows Betty. She's the friend you hate because her house proves it *can* be done. If you're willing to put in the time she does, that is. In high school Betty wasn't the smartest in the class but she studied for two hours every day and always made the honor roll. You couldn't really call her shy, but it's hard to get close to her. (One reason she doesn't like cleaning women is that they always seem to impose their problems on her.) Betty is really quite pretty—her lipstick is always on straight and her medicine chest is filled with creams and lotions that she uses in a twenty-minute beauty ritual every morning and night. She dresses neatly, if a bit unimaginatively, and no one can recall seeing her with her slip showing or a run in her stocking. Betty always takes the trouble to be on time for a lunch date with her friends, and no telephone company ever had to send her a second reminder.

Betty is up every morning at dawn, but she never gets it all done either. Her home is a marvel; everything gleams. Last night she stayed up till midnight polishing the silver for a dinner party even though it was polished just last week. All her friends envy the way her house looks, but the first thing she says when someone walks in the door is, "I'm sorry everything's such a mess." Betty tries every new product that comes on the market in the hope that it will do the job better. She's convinced she *could* do a much better job, although she spends most of her day cleaning and cooking and, when she has some time to spare, running up new curtains for the kitchen. Betty's husband never complains about the way the house looks, although he does regret her constant straightening up of the papers on his desk.

Sometimes Betty thinks she should get out more and do things but, as she says, "I'm a homemaker first and I enjoy it. I know it pleases my husband to come home to a clean house."

Happiness for Betty is nothing short of perfection, but the pursuit of perfection is so exhausting that she often finds herself tired and bewildered. She will *never* be able to reach the impossible goals she sets for herself and, unless she takes a long hard look at how perfect she is in comparison with everyone else, she'll die with her rubber gloves on. Betty may have as many doubts about her ability to be a good homemaker as Marjorie has but she buries them in Lestoil, lotions, and lists.

If you're a Betty, it's tempting to tell you that this book isn't for you. If you're reasonably content and your family doesn't seem to mind your preoccupation with housework, all we can promise is that you may find some better ways to do old things and some new things to do that you never even thought of. If, however, you find yourself often tired or depressed about the house, perhaps you should measure your home against those of your friends and not against an imagined, idealized standard. Since you have tremendous organizational talents and an ability to get things done properly, you'd be an asset to any organization or office. You might try doing equally well something that isn't connected with your house. But of course there's the danger that you'll do it in addition, instead of instead.

Most of us don't fall into a type anymore neatly than we keep our houses. It's likely that you've already discovered that, although you're mostly a Marjorie, you're an awful lot like Betty, with a sprinkle of Daphne thrown in. That doesn't make you a split personality, just a rather normal woman. For reasons of your own, which may not be as simple as you think, you want to improve as homemaker, housekeeper, wife, slave, or whatever your pet name for your job happens to be.

And your house is probably not nearly as badly run as Marjorie's, Daphne's, or Topsy's. In fact, after reading about them, you may wonder why you spend a disproportionate amount of your time wishing you did a better job and worrying about your inability to be a perfect homemaker.

II

Why You're Crazy

Different as Marjorie and Topsy and Daphne and Betty are, they, and you, and everyone else have at least one thing in common. They're taking care of their houses in less than optimum fashion. It's awfully unlikely that you could find someone who was perfect in every way, but who did a terrible job of keeping house. The probability is vast that they, and you, mess up their lives in other areas. The question is why. And it's not a very easy question to answer.

It would be futile to try to convince you all at once that the whole problem is that you want to sleep with your father and kill your mother. Let's start with something simple like, would you believe that sometimes you're unhappy? Good. Now try swallowing this. When you're unhappy you have certain special ways of your own of cheering yourself up and making yourself feel better.

You could try thinking of your head sort of like the Constitution of the United States—a system of checks and balances. Imagine for a moment that you're single. (If you're not.) Let's say everything's been going along just fine. You've gotten out of college with no more than your share of hangups, you're not given to long periods of shutting yourself up in your room and counting all the flowers on your wallpaper; you have enough dates, compared to the rest of your friends; you maintain reasonably cordial relations with your parents (provided they don't insist on seeing you more than once a month); you're doing nicely in your job. In short, you function pretty well (although you frequently think you could be doing better) and nobody can point at you and say, "Gee whiz, old Marcia must be bananas. Do you realize she hasn't left her apartment for the last three months?" Okay. So all of a sudden, your fiancé decides that he is, at thirty-six, far too young to get married, and anyway he has decided to quit his job as assistant associate advertising manager at International Floating Figleaf, Inc., to join a pornographic rock group. Check. Upset.

So you balance (make yourself get happier) by going out and meticulously eating your way through all thirty-one flavors in one weekend, gaining five pounds, and then having a short fling with someone you picked up at a May Day Rally to free Chester Allen Arthur, a cause to which you've taken to devoting three evenings a week. You begin to spend half of your day at the office making long lists of all the people you're going to invite to a fund-raising costume party to free Chester A. Arthur, along with a neatly ruled column for their preference in ice-cream flavors and another for the costume you think they'd be likely to wear. That's your balance, and it keeps you from brooding over what's bothering you.

Of course, what sometimes happens is that you get unbalanced. Suppose you figure somewhere in your head that if one affair and five pounds made you feel less upset, then fifteen pounds and three affairs will make you feel positively euphoric. Then the balance turns into a check and you find yourself fat and promiscuous and unemployed and in jail when it turns out that Chester A. Arthur is really Mao Tse-tung. You're so guilty and depressed by now that even joining the Peace Corps or going into a convent doesn't help, and you are truly monumentally hung up.

All the things you do serve the very useful purpose of keeping your head above water, that is, they keep the anxiety, depression, and unhappiness that you inevitably feel at times from breaking out in really destructive and unacceptable ways.

So, if you can accept that you have conscious conflicts that you have to resolve if you want to avoid unhappiness and that you have conscious ways of resolving them, it may not be too difficult for you to accept the idea that you might also have unconscious conflicts and unconscious ways of coping with them.

In either case, you need a field on which to use the ways you have of coping and, if you're a housewife, full- or part-time, it stands to reason that your house might provide a very handy one. (This may explain many cases in which a woman has absolutely no trouble keeping up her house until she changes her life style in some way—gets married, has a baby, for instance, or quits a job. In changing her life style she's giving up some areas which were previously used as a field on which to work out her problems.) And besides, there are all sorts of very real things that have to do with being a housewife and taking care of a house that cause conscious and unconscious conflicts and unhappiness of their own.

We are now going to attempt to explain, in relatively heavy psychiatric terms, why it is that you don't always do things in your own best interest. Why you might eat an ice-cream sundae even though you know that losing twenty pounds is infinitely preferable, or why you might spend the afternoon reading *True Romances* (or, for that matter, *An Introduction to Nuclear Physics*) when you know bloody well that what you should be doing is washing the kitchen floor.

VERY HEAVY PSYCHIATRIC STUFF WHICH YOU MAY SKIP IF YOU DON'T FEEL UP TO IT

There's something to be said for the theory that basically all anyone wants to do is to be like a baby, and sleep and eat. That's what you're born with, and it's hard to overcome. When a baby can't get food, he gets angry and he cries. When he gets a little older, when he can't get when he wants, he gets angry and he cries (or he hits Mommy, or he breaks something). Mommies don't like that. So mommies teach babies that they have to control their aggressive impulses and that there are better ways of working things out. Mommies and Daddies have also discovered that if they left you to your own devices, you'd grow up to be Godzilla or maybe, if they were very lucky, Jerry Rubin. So they start to teach you the difference between right and wrong. Sociologically or philosophically this is called imparting morals. Looked at psychiatrically, it might be called clamping down on the id.

The id is the part of you that, left to its own devices, would do whatever was fun, pleasurable, gratifying, or turn-onny, without regard to consequences. Unfortunately (or fortunately, if you assume that there's some value to be gained in promoting our difference from the common tree frog who only wants to eat and sleep) some restraints have to be imposed.

Here you have this little kid who wants what it wants and whose Mommy and Daddy want what they want—and who do you think is going to win? Actually both. Remember, as much as a kid wants to do anything without restriction, he also loves his Mommy and Daddy and he wants to make them happy and he wants to be like them.

Suppose a two-year-old grabs a cookie from the

cookie jar. His mother gives him a whack and tells him not to take things. The second time it happens, his mother gives him a whack and tells him not to take things. The third time he goes to the cookie jar he says, "I'd better not take a cookie because if I do Mommy will spank me." But, if his parents are doing their job right, the fourth time he says to himself, "I'm not hungry." He's being good not just out of fear of a hurt bottom. He's made the undesirability of lifting cookies a part of himself. Being good and doing good things leak into him slowly until they have become a part of him, and this is the start of his superego.

A superego is the incorporation of parental (or societal) feelings of what's right. It is, as you'll see constantly at war with the self-serving infantile pressure of the id. Since the two- or five- or seven-year-old sees his parents as gods on whom to model himself, he is going to mimic their behavior, as well as follow their verbal promptings. So, if Daddy keeps telling him that he shouldn't lift things from the five-and-ten and every night Daddy tells everyone at the dinner table how he's embezzled another fifty thousand at the bank, junior is apt to be confused. This is why child-rearing books are always telling you to be consistent.

So the start of conflict begins with the two-year-old who wants that cookie like crazy with one part of him (his id) and with another part of him (his superego) doesn't want to want it like crazy. Like crazy is how he's going to go unless he finds a way to deal with two very strong conflicting desires—not only a way to decide between them, but a way to keep his id and his superego happy at the same time. When a conflict can't be resolved, in a child or in an adult, it causes anxiety—for which you may read tension or depression or disequilibrium or guilt or hostility—at any rate, a not very happy feeling. Nobody wants that, let alone a two-year-old, so you develop something that keeps you together. That something is called the ego.

You could think of the ego as a kind of computer that sits in your head and decides who's going to get it this time. (If you thought of it that way you wouldn't be exactly right, but it's close enough for what is certainly the most simplistic explanation of Freudian theory yet promulgated.) It checks out the situation, applies everything that you've ever learned, tests reality, as it were, and puts the brakes on the id when it feels the superego has the better case. If you have what is known in the jargon as an especially punitive superego, it doesn't let you have very much fun.

The way the ego puts the brakes on the id in a way that keeps you from feeling miserable all the time is by using a whole lot of devices that are called defense mechanisms. One of the most common defense mechanisms, and the one that's used almost exclusively by children under the age of six, is called *repression,* which can best be explained by going back to the little kid and the cookie jar. Faced with the intolerable situation, the ego repressed the desire before it even got up to the kid's consciousness, so that the effect was a child who said, and totally believed, "I wasn't hungry anyway."

When you do that sort of thing on a conscious level, like when Marjorie doesn't wax the kitchen floor because she says to herself that it's far more important to get out the vote, you're not repressing, you're *rationalizing.* When you have an unacceptable feeling about something, say you're very mad at your two-month-old baby because he's kept you up all night, but it doesn't seem quite fair to take it out on your poor defenseless baby, and consciously or unconsciously you get mad at your mother and have a fight with her, you're *displacing.* When you have feelings that are unacceptable to you, like wanting to hit your husband over the head with the nearest blunt object, you may find other ways to get rid of your hostility—like painting a picture or kicking the dog—which is called *sub-limating*.

What complicates things is that a child's ego is very good at repressing unconscious fantasies or desires that are unacceptable, but it can only repress them, not legislate them out of existence. And there they may sit for the rest of his life unless some apparently irrelevant situation brings them bobbing up from the unconscious. So frequently, when you act in a fashion that seems less than reasonable to you, what may be happening is that some hoary old fantasy from when you were a little kid has been activated, and your ego, being ever considerate of your mental health and not wanting to bother you with such a painful conflict, finds ways of keeping it down that are not always consistent with doing the right thing at the right time.

So, while it's easy to say that any grown-up should be able to make up her own mind and behave rationally, unfortunately having grown to precipitous adulthood, you've brought along all sorts of baggage, all sorts of strong id-motivated wishes that never got granted and that are intolerable to your superego. This may affect your ability to act at all times in your own best interests, because your ego, seeking to spare you unpleasantness, will resort to fair means or foul to keep that old anxiety and so forth from welling up to the surface. Thus, if, as a child, you wanted to kill your mother and sleep with your father, although your ego repressed the desire and slapped it into your unconscious, you might meet a man someday who reminds you of your father and you may feel that you have to defend against the same unacceptable desires you had as a dirty little girl. (Or you might marry him, thus helping you to resolve your Oedipal conflict.) Of course it doesn't always have to be a nasty fantasy. If you never worked out your tremendous conflict over cookies, you may feel very threatened at the sight of a cookie.

One more thing, and then we'll proceed with what this actually has to do with why your house is a mess. Children, as you know if you've spent any time with them, are different from you and me. For one thing, they have some trouble separating out what's imaginary from what's real (they aren't quite sure whether the monsters they see on the television set are capable of eating them up or not; if they have a dream about lions coming to kill them, it's hard to convince them that there aren't really any lions in their bedroom). This louses them up when it comes to figuring out cause and effect. So if every night when your mommy tucked you in she was especially loving and always wore the same perfume, you might grow up with a nice feeling about that perfume. Or if every time you saw your parents fighting you saw them sitting in the same two turquoise chairs, you might have a kind of antipathy toward furnishing your living room with turquoise chairs. Okay. Now on to what this all has to do with anything and what you can do about it.

How the Junk in Your Head May Be the Cause of the Mess on the Floor and Vice Versa

YOU MAY HAVE SPECIFIC FANTASIES ABOUT SPECIFIC OBJECTS

Since we talked about that last, we'll talk about it first, since it's still fresh in your head. If you harbor unconscious memories that associate turquoise chairs with fighting, you may not only avoid buying turquoise chairs, but you may avoid cleaning anything in your house that's turquoise, because it makes unpleasant memories come bobbing up. Or let's say that you once saw your mother shriek after she'd gotten a terrible electric shock from the vacuum. It might put you off vacuums. Or they once read you a story where a princess turned into a frog because she didn't make her bed. It might have made you so concerned about making beds that you started changing your linens every day so you wouldn't turn into a frog. (There's not a single solitary thing I can do to help you out of these absolutely absurd notions which you inevitably hold. That's what analysis is for—after three years, you realize that you make your bed every day because you're afraid you'll turn into a frog if you don't, and your analyst points out to you that this is a pretty dumb way to feel, considering that you're thirty years old and no one you know has ever turned into a frog, and you don't really believe it—then *voilà!* You are now able to leave off changing your sheets every day.)

Starting from those relatively far-fetched examples, let's try to see how you can louse up your housekeeping for two reasons.

1. The very nature of housekeeping is such that it causes conflicts that have to be resolved if you want to avoid being unhappy.
2. Your home is a very handy place on which to exercise your own particular means of avoiding discomfort from other areas.

YOUR HOUSEKEEPING IS A FUNCTION OF YOUR ROLE AS A WOMAN

And you may be in conflict about what your role as a woman really should be. Women's liberation, right? To a major degree, your superego defines for you what your role involves. It makes you feel uncomfortable if you want to become President of the United States, because you were taught as a child that aggressiveness, masculinity, and so forth were unacceptable feelings in a little girl and your parents frowned on them, so you repressed them. Now, when they crop up you feel conflict between the desire to do what you want and the desire to do what you think you should. Making a bed, then, may bring up the conflict because it forces you to decide between doing what you want to and doing what you've been taught.

If you dislike your particular role, your dislike may manifest itself in a dislike of and disinclination to deal with any of the trappings. If you hate your sink because of the work it makes you do, you may take it out directly on the sink and not do anything for it.

The problem of the woman who works and has a husband and/or kids is rather more complex. For one thing, she has to be reassessing her role constantly. If she's having a rotten time at work, it's relatively easy to rationalize things by saying, "What the hell, it's my role as wife and/or mother that really matters." On the other hand, if she hates a lot of things about her role as wife and/or mother, it's a short step to thinking along the lines of "My job is more important than a lousy kitchen floor and I would be a rotten, unhappy person and no good to my husband and children if I didn't work," and proceed to neglect things around the house on the basis of too much doing at work. You don't even have to be married. Single women who haven't quite worked out in their heads whether they want the rose-covered cottage or the wall-to-wall carpeted office may swing back and forth while they're deciding. Finding a woman who works and has a family who is consistently able to function optimally in both roles (I said optimally) isn't too usual. Switching back and forth can be hard.

For some reason, the question of cooking seems to fit in here (actually it could be that I'm hungry). There are a remarkable number of women who loathe everything that has to do with cleaning a house and revel in turning themselves into gourmet cooks. I tend to think this is some kind of complicated copout—although I hasten to add that I fall squarely into the Julia-Child-in-the-kitchen-Phyllis-Diller-in-the-living-room school of thought and action—I offer several reasons for this. First of all, it's a way of defining your role—the obvious thing of single girl showing suitor what marvelous wife material she would make, or young-wife-shows-husband-what-good-choice-he-made.

But I think there's somewhat more to it. Take for instance a mother faced with a kid who doesn't eat. She has to be pretty secure to stand it. After all, it is the first and probably the most important physical demonstration of caring for a child. His failure to eat is not only an insult to your cooking ability, which is bad enough, or a symbolic rejection of you and your love, but you may view it as an affront to your ability as a mother—which is all tied up with those nasty conflicts about your role and how well you're playing it. Not to mention what they say about mothers with scrawny children—it's bad public relations. So a mother with a child who doesn't eat may feel very threatened.

For a child, as for you, there's a tremendous equation between food and love and, unless he learns to divorce the two to a reasonable degree, he may grow up taking the one when he can't get the other and being fat. This is gross oversimplification, and it doesn't mean that fat people are all miserably insecure. On the other hand, why do people in love often lose their appetites?

Then there's the whole question of creativity. There is, for many women, something distinctly satisfying about bringing forth a full-course meal of which every last nutmeg-dusted side dish has been made from scratch. Even if it does get destroyed in an hour, it existed as something created or made by you as opposed to cleaning—which is a mere removal of dirt and only a creation if one considers the creation of order as real and concrete.

This brings us, I'm not exactly sure how, to something else about cooking that intrigues me. Is there some relationship between women who leave their kitchens looking as though the Battle of Bull Run had been fought and lost there, and people whose desks resemble the streets of downtown New York after the astronauts paraded through? It could be that in both cases the image that's being put across is one of "see how hard I am working." So a woman who cooks a lot and cooks with a messy kitchen may possibly be in conflict about her role as a housewife in more ways than one.

CONSIDER YOUR COMPETITION

Maybe it's partly your friends that you're comparing yourself with, but a rather important personage also enters into it, if you think about it—your mom. Now at first this may seem absurd, as in many cases you're a distinctly better housewife than your mother. But it's not the mother that you visited in her less than immaculate nest last week that you're seeing. It's the mother you saw when you were three or seven or nine— a fantastic lady who cooked, cleaned, sewed, and dispensed love and cookies infinitely better than you could *then*. She was supermother—and even though the years have cut her down to size to your conscious eye, part of you still may see her as you did then. Or as my son says to me, "Mommy, you make the very best Jello." (By the way, that may be why you'll never be as good a cook as your mother-in-law. Nothing tastes as good as it does when you're six years old and hungry.) So one problem may be that you find it difficult to housekeep because part of you believes you'll never be as good as your mother and that's what you feel you have to live up to.

Another part of you may be not so sure you want to be better than your mother. It's a very common fantasy to want to replace your mother. If you can swallow the idea that you once wanted to get rid of your mother so you could spend all of your time with your Daddy, you can see that surpassing her in house-keeping may threaten you. It may seem to your sub-conscious that it's too reminiscent of those old un-acceptable fantasies of wanting to do away with her. So you may not want to let yourself get better than she is. This fear of success can easily come up in other areas. You could stay fat, even though it didn't make any sense, because deep down being fat made you unattractive to men and made it impossible to act out your fantasies about wanting to sleep with your father.

A HOUSE IS A VERY HANDY PLACE TO FIND THINGS TO DO THAT MAKE YOU FEEL BETTER

Let's suppose that you're Betty and you've just had some bad news. Scrubbing sidewalks in front of her house may make Betty feel a lot better because it takes her mind off her problems. Or let's suppose you're Marjorie and you've had some bad news and you were intending to scrub the sidewalk. But it makes Marjorie feel better to rearrange the magazines, so she does that instead. The things that you find to do that make you feel better are not necessarily the things that should be done. (This may help to explain why you do things that are terribly unnecessary instead of doing necessary things. It may not be merely a dislike for washing the kitchen floor that makes you rearrange your husband's undershirts—it may be a need to do something like arranging undershirts in order to keep you from think-ing about some terribly extraneous depressing thing. Of course, if it happened that you were supposed to arrange your husband's undershirts, you can see where this might sometimes turn out to be a positive force for good.)

A HOUSE IS A VERY GOOD PLACE TO TAKE OUT HOSTILITY THAT YOU MAY NOT BE ABLE TO TAKE OUT DIRECTLY

You may feel anger at your husband or at your family that may have a lot or a little or nothing to do with the demands they make on your housework. Since the idea of behaving aggressively toward them is hard to take, you may sublimate your hostility either in fairly direct ways—like not sending your husband's suit to the cleaner, or forgetting to keep Jello around when you know your children adore it. Or you may neglect things in a more overall and diffuse way.

A HOUSE IS A RELATIVELY INNOC-UOUS PLACE TO GET RID OF SOME OF THE GUILT AND DEPRESSION YOU MAY BE FEELING IN A MORE THREATENING AREA

Assuming that your ego isn't perfect and that you're going to experience guilt from time to time, it's a lot easier to feel guilty over your inadequacy as a cleaning woman than it is to feel guilty over your real or imagined failure as a wife or mother or person. It's much easier to berate yourself for not emptying a wastebasket than it is to dwell on why you yelled at your child for doing something that wasn't his fault, or why you haven't read a good book since college. So sitting in a chair and reading a book and feeling miserable about the house is a good deal more pleasant than washing a kitchen floor and feeling miserable about something a lot more real or threatening. You can apply the above to depression as well. If you're disturbed because your ego couldn't figure out some way to keep you from having a big conflict over something, then you may find it easier to get depressed about your dirty bathroom. Incidentally, one sure-fire sign of depression is an inability to do *anything*. Which could be a way of dealing with some terrible conflict by saying, if I don't do anything then I don't have much of a chance of doing this terrible thing I want to do. Or if I don't feel anything, then I won't feel this terrible thing that I feel.

Of course, there are probably loads of other reasons why you may have some difficulty in shouldering your burden. But I think that's enough for now, anyway. To make the whole thing a bit more graphic, let's look at a situation that may not be too foreign from some experience of your own.

A SITUATION THAT MAY NOT BE TOO FOREIGN FROM SOME EXPERIENCE OF YOUR OWN

Let's suppose you've been brooding a lot lately about the fact that your husband isn't making enough money, and you decide the next day that you'll clean out his closet for him. You wouldn't *believe* the things that might lie behind this simple act. In the first place, you may be cleaning that closet out of what the shrinks call reaction formation (you haven't felt *consciously* hostile, but you have subconsciously and you're doing something nice to make up for those nasty subconscious fantasies you've had about doing him in). Or your old ego, struggling to defend against feelings of depression, is using the wonderfully obsessive-compulsive act of cleaning out a closet to help you along. Or, in getting rid of some of your husband's old things you may be displacing, and finding an acceptable way of expressing your unconscious desire to get rid of him. Nevertheless, all you know as you fall into bed after an exhausting day is that you did a nice thing for him, you cleaned out his closet.

However, as you lie comatose on your pillow that night your husband casually tosses a little goodie at you like, "Say darling, how come you never get the ring out of the bathtub?" It is remarkable how many fights get started this way. You feel:

1. For God's sake, I spent the whole day cleaning out the rotten closets, including *his* rotten closet, and he doesn't even mention it. (Hostility.)

2. Why the hell can't he clean out the bloody ring in the tub if he cares so much about it? He never helps me anyway. (Hostility.)

3. He doesn't appreciate me.

4. If I'd married Fred who now owns a chain of bowling alleys, I'd have a full-time maid. If he got killed in an automobile accident I could marry Fred. . . . (Unacceptable fantasy.)

5. (A whiney little voice piping up from your subconscious) "I'm a lousy wife." (Depression.) Depressed people often get angry. They do not always get angry at themselves.

6. I *should* keep the bathtub clean. (Guilt.)

Your husband feels:

1. For God's sake, I worked hard at the office (or coal mine or whatever) all day. Is it too much to expect a goddam clean bathtub which my mother always had? (Hostility: unacceptable fantasy about wanting to sleep with his mother.)

2. Why the devil is she so tired? So big deal, she cleaned out my closet and now I'll never be able to find anything. (Hostility.)

3. I bet she's not even going to want to screw tonight. (Hostility.)

4. If I'd married Gloria she'd probably keep the house spotless and I bet she'd be a better lay. (Unacceptable fantasy.)

5. (That little subconscious again): "If I were better at what I did I could afford to get her a maid and we wouldn't have these problems." (Guilt.)

6. I'm rotten. (Depression.)

(Of course you have conveniently forgotten that Fred is tied up with the Mafia in addition to being homosexual. And your husband has equally forgotten that Gloria's husband is sharing old Gloria with the entire Wednesday-night poker game.)

Now one couple in a hundred or a hundred thousand will resolve this in a reasonable way, because all the conscious and unconscious crud that's mucking about in the background obscures the issue.

You: "Gee, I'm sorry dear. I was so hung up on cleaning the closets I didn't get to the bathroom. I didn't realize it bugged you so much."

He: "Oh, never mind. I can do it myself and really thanks for cleaning out my closet. It's a joy to be able to find things in it."

Kiss . . . Dissolve. . . .

The other 99,999 will get involved in a dialogue along these lines:

You: "Listen, goddammit, I spent the whole lousy day cleaning out the closets and I'm exhausted and why can't you do something around here for a change?"

He: "*Do* something around here? What did I do all day Saturday, for Chrissake, hanging pictures and fixing the leak and God knows what."

You: "So you spent a couple of hours on Saturday. If you hadn't been drunk at that office party, you'd have gotten that promotion and I'd have a maid by now."

He: "You seem to forget that the boss heard you telling someone he was an old lecher."

Go ahead and fill in the blanks. But remember, you've come a long way from the ring in the bathtub, baby.

Since so few marriages survive through a week of one crisis on top of another without a fight struggling to get itself born, I give you the following totally artificial rule, which may help things from getting out of hand.

Never fight in the bedroom.

If you develop a hard and fast rule to fight only in the living room (or, if you live in a one-room apartment, you could agree to fight only in the bathroom, which would make for probably fewer fights and anyway more interesting ones when they happened) you might see some advantages:

1. Your sex life won't get screwed up because you'll be able to make a distinction between and a transition between fighting and making love.

2. The whole action of moving a fight, if it starts in the bedroom, to the living room, may be enough of a physical pause to keep things from escalating unmercifully.

3. If you live in an apartment, you will give less to the neighbors to talk about, since voices generally tend to lower in the living room. And you will give less to your kids to be traumatized about, since they will be less likely to hear you.

4. You will be somewhat more civilized, since sitting in a chair is slightly less elemental than lying in a bed.

5. You will cut the risk of falling asleep during an especially loud and/or protracted fight. Some people react to a fight by dropping out of the unpleasantness completely, which for some peculiar reason infuriates their opponent.

Ultimately, one is faced with the question of whether one should become a better housewife. After all, we've shown that displacing things onto your house serves a generally useful purpose—helping to keep you from going crazy. It offers lots of nifty ways to use your own particular ways of getting rid of things that bother you. It keeps you from killing your husband and children and maybe yourself; it keeps you from feeling guilty about what a really rotten person you are deep down. So maybe you shouldn't improve. You may be taking away one of the best outlets your ego has to work with. Who *knows* where else it might be forced to look?

On the other hand, even assuming that you may never be able to clean lamps because they're phallic and that brings up all sorts of fantasies about sleeping with your father, and since it's probable that you won't go beserk, there may be some ways to improve.*

Whether you're a little bothered or very upset, there are some things that you can do that might help.

1. You can make a stab at getting to the root of what's really bothering you, by thinking about things. I've suggested some possibilities and I'm sure you can think of more.

2. If you think you know what's bugging you, you can try talking about it—what's called in the trade "ventilating." Sometimes it helps and sometimes it doesn't, but keeping everything locked up inside can cause ulcers as well as broken vases.

3. If you're feeling hostility, you can try expressing some of it. Really, not cleaning the ring in the bathtub and complaining about the ring are marital sins so small as to rank with forgetting to put a salad fork on the table at dinner time. If you're into a fight, you can try to get down to some of the things that are really bothering you. Getting down to the nitty gritty is often very threatening. It is, however, something to strive for.

* If you are in analysis, consult with your physician before embarking on this plan.

4. You can look for other ways to sublimate. Obviously you have to look around pretty carefully, but if you could invest a good part of yourself in something else—a job, perhaps, or, don't laugh, a hobby, you could take some things out there.

5. (And this is where the whole rest of the book comes in.) You can create a situation in which it's harder to sublimate and displace all over your house by ordering your house—keeping it finite. As we mentioned way back in the first chapter, housekeeping is a very attractive outlet because it is so undefined as to allow for a great deal of working things out, not always to the advantage of your house. Very briefly, I will explain how we're going to go about it:

First, by using one of your more resilient ego functions, reality testing, you can determine exactly how terrible a job you're actually doing. Just knowing that may help.

Second, there's a nifty reality test for figuring out exactly what's involved in doing a good job of housekeeping in your particular case. This should help to make you set realistic goals, thus cutting out one surefire means of built-in failure, as well as finding out precisely what you should and shouldn't be doing.

Third, we offer a way to make the demands even more finite by showing you how to schedule yourself so that your time is structured and doesn't allow for any random displacement.

Fourth, we've got one very simple plan for bringing order out of chaos and a lot of ideas on how you can order your house physically so that you can't work out your own inside chaos on it.

Fifth, we're going to tackle one of the most common problems that cause your housework to be infinite—lack of knowledge about how to do things.

I'm not promising that this will work. I'm just saying that it might. The principle, if you want to be graphic, is that if you remove most of the temptation to louse things up, things should get better. Think of how easy it would be to go on a diet if they locked you up in a room without any food.

III

How to Change Your Life, Achieve Marital Happiness, Amaze Friends and Family With Your Efficiency, Give Up All Those Crazy Ideas About Baking Fresh Bread... and Find Out Once and For All Just Exactly How Rotten a Housekeeper You Are

Reality Test Number 1

How Bad a Housekeeper Are You Actually?
Rate your house on a scale of 1 to 10 (using 1 as a ravaged pesthole and 10 as absolutely spotless. Nobody gets a 10 unless people can eat off the top of the furnace). Think of it the way it is most of the time, not after it's been cleaned up for company.

Get a pad and write down your Basic Rating.

Now add points for each of the following that applies:

Baby under one year	add 1
Child one year to nursery school	add 2
Child in nursery school, but not a full day	add 2
Child in school full day	add 1
Twins	add 2
Triplets	add 3
Days you work	add 1 for each
Days you have a maid	subtract 1 for each
Days spent in charity work or other meaningful unpaid work (include time as unpaid help to husband's business)	add ½ for each day
No children at all	subtract 3
No husband	subtract 3
Rooms, under 5	subtract ½ for each
Rooms, over 5	add ½ for each
Live in a house	add 1
Live in an apartment	subtract 1

True or false

Despite what I think of my house, my husband and family rarely or ever complain	add 1 if true

Now, total it all up.

HOW TO SCORE

1 to 3	It's really as bad as you thought, if not worse. You're a horrible housekeeper.
3 to 4	Although you'll never win any awards, there do exist numerous women throughout the world whose houses are in far worse shape than yours.
5	All things considered, you're about average, which is not to be laughed at.
6 to 7	You're a lot better than most. Really.
8 to 9	You're an excellent housekeeper. Congratulations.
10 or over	You're so incredibly good that you should take this book back to the store and ask for a refund.

That's how you rate relative to everybody. However, that may not mean a damn thing to you if you still think that everybody does a better job than you do. If that's your problem, rate three or four of your friends on the same scale, making sure you rate all houses as they appear under similar conditions. Then compare their final score with yours. In fact, why don't you rate your mother-in-law in this fashion? You might find out that, all things considered, you do a lot better job than she does.

Hopefully, the results of that test should have reassured you. Or at least let you know a bit more realistically where you stand. No matter how badly you scored on the Housekeeper test, there is hope for you, as there is for Marjorie, Daphne, Topsy, and Betty (and even for you, Virginia, as soon as you stop believing that Santa Claus is going to come down the chimney and wash down your walls). On the other hand, if you scored high, that's fantastic. It should keep you from getting uptight about the house. But there are those of us who can be holding down a job, raising two-year-old triplets, refinishing the basement, and who still get all upset if our house isn't as shiny as the widow lady's next door who has three in live-in help. Unfortunate as that is, it's not uncommon. Just keep reading.

It is, by the way, one of the myths perpetrated against new brides that there will be *something* you enjoy doing. Perhaps you will enjoy ironing, or maybe washing woodwork will be your thing. But somehow, something about keeping house is supposed to turn you on. I personally never found a thing I enjoy about cleaning house, with the exception of arranging roses in crystal vases.

Actually, the chances are immense that the major problem facing you is not so much lack of enthusiasm or rampant disorganization, or fear of the color brown, but rather that of faulty reality testing. If you're suffering from nagging faulty reality testing you have probably noticed the following symptoms:

1. You're not doing the right job at the right time.
2. You're not doing the right job the right way.

At this point, I rather think some of you are saying to yourselves, "Well, that's absolutely true, but what good can that possibly do? She's probably going to tell me that I should just put on my prettiest house-dress, drink a cup of tea in my best Melmac tea cup in my living room, and push on."

Certainly not. We're not going to cure you by attacking the problem at the source (like it probably makes a tremendous difference how old you were when your mother started toilet training you, but you probably don't remember and mothers are such notoriously bad reporters of their children's development that if they were to be believed, the present generation of children would have to be considered severely mentally retarded, since everyone I know was walking at three months and doing integral calculus by four, according to their mothers). But we're going to attack the problem symptomatically.*

So essentially, we're going to perform some radical psychotherapy on your housekeeping problems by teaching you to reality test about yourself and your house.

---

* This in a nutshell, in case you've been wondering and nobody could ever tell you in under twenty-five thousand poly-syllabic words, is the difference between psychotherapy and psychoanalysis. In psychoanalysis, which usually involves four to five hours a week, they try to find out what fantasies you had when you were very little that made you grow up acting like such an idiot, then knowing that, let you learn that the things that happened to you when you were little weren't really all that important, so you should stop acting like an idiot. In psychotherapy, which usually takes one to three hours a week, they recognize that you're acting like an idiot and try to show you ways in which you could stop acting like an idiot. My husband says his stomach hurts after reading that.

FOR WHOM DO YOU KEEP HOUSE, ANYWAY?

Probably, to some extent or another for
1) Strangers
2) Your friends (if you happen to have any)
3) Other relatives
4) Your children (if you happen to have any)
5) Your husband (if you happen to have one)
6) You

Take them one by one and consider. If the house displeases:

1) Strangers

Unless Mrs. Henry Parrish II and Billy Baldwin have just decorated your home and *House Beautiful* is coming to photograph it, or the adoption agency is coming to check you out, or the President of the United States is looking over your place with an eye to renting it for the summer, rare are the strangers who will be put off by an only reasonably clean house.

2) Friends

Ditto. In fact, some of your friends may secretly love you for being a slob. (Cultivate a slob. Visit her whenever your house gets you down. Do not under any circumstances lend her this book.)

3) Relatives

Few, if any, are the mothers-in-law who will turn their sons against you because of a dirty oven. As long as he appears to be reasonably well fed and clothed and is not seeing the shrink any more than when he was living at home, she hasn't got much of a case. Actually, it gives her a chance to gripe to her bridge group about you and to convince herself that she was right about you all the time in just about the most harmless way possible. As for other relatives, well, what the hell. Do you really care? Really? Why? Really, really?

4) Your children

Couldn't care less provided that, if they're teenagers, their house is not several hundred times worse than their friends' houses; if they're little kids, that they can find their toys, at least most of the time. Offhand I can think of at least forty ways of expressing love for children that are more meaningful than Windexing their mirrors.

5) Your husband (for which you may read your lover or the man you are going to marry, or for that matter your roommate, if it is important that you please her/him, in which case you might ask yourself why it is so important that you please her/him).

Most husbands do not give a damn about the state of your lingerie drawer, provided you don't come to bed on your anniversary in a nightgown with holes. They don't care where you keep the preserves, whether the tops of the kitchen cabinets have been cleaned in the last five years, or if the poetry section of your bookshelves is arranged by author or title. Instead, they care about things directly relating to their comfort. Such as:

clean sheets on the bed
clean windows to look out of
clean laundry in their drawers
clean children on their laps (that is, no unappealing and readily apparent material in their diapers—most people wouldn't know if you bathed your kids once a day or once a year, provided you kept after them with a soapy washcloth)
soap in the bathtub
lights in the lamps
beer in the refrigerator
you in bed

Most, not all but most, people are far more concerned with organization than with cleanliness. Specifically, a lack of debris and the ability to find something in its accustomed place when it's needed is all most people care about, assuming the degree of air pollution in the house doesn't creep past the danger level.

Most men are not as sensitive to dirt as their wives, and most can tolerate a relatively large amount of clutter, provided it doesn't impinge on their preserves. On the other hand, it's by no means inconceivable that your husband may be making unrealistic demands on you as a housekeeper, which we will get to later. But, for the purpose of reality testing, we'll make the assumption that, since so much conflict arises over your failure to do something around the house that's important to your husband, it may be useful to find out what he cares about.

6) You

If you get right down to it, what you care about, without regard to the opinions of others, is probably rather limited. Reflect on that for a minute. This is not to say that you shouldn't keep the top of the piano dusted if you've noticed that your mother-in-law runs her finger along the top of it to check for dust every time she comes to visit. It is, however, a mistake to assume that just because she's hung up on your dusty piano that she's necessarily going to check out your medicine chest.

If literally *all* your friends have clean bathrooms and yours bears an unpleasant resemblance to the ones you've passed up on the New Jersey Turnpike, is the lack of conformity to neighborhood standards reason enough to be bothered? Clear one-to-one comparisons are generally rare and more painful than more diffuse ones. That is, it's harder to face up to the fact that you have the dirtiest bathroom in town than it is to say, "Now, let's see, my kitchen is cleaner than Sue's and my bathroom is dirtier than Ann's but it's cleaner than Sue's and my silver is never as shiny as Barbara's but on the other hand my china doesn't have little bits of egg sticking to it."

Only God, and maybe your analyst, knows what's behind your desperate need to keep the kitchen floor spotlessly clean while the bathtub languishes and grows green. But in an effort to find out what really matters, we offer

Reality Test Number 2

What the Devil Do You Think You're Doing?

List A

Take a pencil and write down ten things that you do around the house that really matter a whole lot (washing the kitchen floor, polishing the furniture, picking up the kids' toys). Leave out things like washing dishes or making beds or flushing the toilet, which almost anyone will admit leave you no choice—they must be done every day.

List B

Now write down ten things that you have been meaning to do or that you feel guilty about not having done. (Actually, there is nothing to prevent you from writing down twenty or fifty or three on each list. You should do your own thing.)

Now ask your husband, or if you can't ask him now, ask him later, to do the same thing and enter his answers below your own. His first list, *List C,* should be things that seem to get done around the house that would bother him if they didn't get done and his second list, *List D,* should be of things he wishes you'd do one of these days. (You must try not to get offended at the nasty things he says, if he says them. Or at the fact that he isn't even aware that you spend whole days polishing the silver. This test has too much significance to be interrupted by a silly fight. Go back and read about hostility again.)

You now should have four neat lists, A, B, C, and D.

Now take another piece of paper and enter items from Lists A and C that are the same, more or less, under a section you will call I.

Under Section II, enter items from Lists B and D that are the same.

Under Section III, enter any items from your lists (A and B) that don't match those in your husband's lists (C and D).

And last, in Section IV enter any items from your husband's lists (C and D) that don't match those in your lists (A and B).

Maybe you ought to go back and read all that over, because if you pay a little attention, it's really very clear. You should have seen it before it got simplified.

How To Score: Look at your Lists, I, II, III, and IV.

I

If you scored high in Section I, you and your husband are relatively well in touch with reality and mostly in agreement about what's okay around your house.* You're also spending a good bit of your time doing what's okay around the house.

II

If you scored high in Section II, you're not doing all that you should, but at least you and your husband agree on what should be done.

III

If you scored high in Section III, do the following:

Go back and cross out any items on Lists A and B that are things done by very few people that you know, or that very few people other than you seem to care

---

* Or maybe you're both out of touch with reality.

much about. Then go back and cross out any item that you care about simply because you think (but don't know) somebody other than you or your immediate family cares about. In other words, cross out any job that is to your mind a little bit nutty. The items you have crossed out are probably irrelevant housework that you are doing for some psychological reason other than that they need doing. You can try to psyche yourself out of them by taking a long hard look at exactly why you change your sheets once a day. On the other hand, as you'll see in the next chapter, you can merely try scrapping it for a while and seeing whether or not you go crazy.

Read the following if you feel very uneasy about having crossed out all those things that mean a lot to you.

Why Does It Bother You?

Let's consider the question of why it matters to you to have a clean house in the first place.

1. First of all, because in reality it's generally nicer to live in pleasant surroundings than in a pigsty.

2. You inevitably judge yourself to one degree or another by the kind of house you keep, since it's an important part of your role.

3. You identify closely with your home and feel that people judge you to some degree by the way your house looks.

All of which are excellent reasons to be concerned and probably would be cause for worry if you didn't feel any of them. But suppose that, even though you know quite rationally that your house is not that much worse than anybody else's and your husband hasn't been giving you any particular heat, you are extraordinarily concerned with the state of your house, and it causes you an uncomfortable amount of unhappiness. You might consider any or all of these causes.

1. You may have an awful lot of hostility that you're taking out on your house and having that hostility in the first place may be the cause of your guilt.

2. You may have an awful lot of things that are bothering you, and sublimating them all over your house may not be quite enough to keep them from coming through.

3. You may be in extreme confusion about your role and the tasks of housekeeping may be causing you to test it too frequently for your own comfort.

4. You may have extraordinary amounts of guilt and depression from other areas that are making themselves felt in extreme guilt and depression over the house.

5. You may be judging yourself far too harshly, using an unrealistic image of your mother as the ideal you have to attain.

6. You may be using real or imagined failure as a housewife as a refuge. You may be saying, "I'd be perfect if only I were a better housekeeper."

7. You may be identifying very closely with your house and at the same time be very worried about what people think of you. Especially, if you crossed out a number of items that you think other people care about.

All right. So whose standards are you putting on it? Keeping house, to trim it down to size a little, should be defined as attending to the realistic needs of the people who live there. Obviously you have to keep up a front for friends, relatives, and strangers. But consider whether or not that front isn't keeping you from taking care of the things that really matter, or causing you to put so much of your time and energy into your house that it detracts from other parts of your life. If, despite all of the above extraordinarily sensible advice, there remain crossed-out items that still seem inordinately important to you, put them back in.

IV

If you scored high in Group IV, unless you have an unusually low Housekeeper Score, go back and cross items out according to the instructions at the top of Group III. Check these items out with your husband, and if he isn't willing to let a good number of them go, you must consider the following:

WHAT IF YOUR HUSBAND IS A MALE CHAUVINIST PIG?

If you genuinely feel that your husband requires a level of housekeeping that is out of keeping with the housekeeping among your friends, you should be able to point this out to him in a relatively civilized fashion. Unfortunately, however, although you know that Gertrude's house looks like the main salon of the *Titanic* just before it went down, except when she's having you and your husband over to dinner, your husband has no way of knowing this. You could jeopardize your friendship with Gertrude and drop in some morning around 9:00 A.M. with your husband. Or you could take your husband on a guided tour of the beauty spots of Gertrude's house when you're there some night. He might respond favorably to being shown the underside of her bed or the linen closet. If you have a real friend in Gertrude you could plot ahead with her. So before you plan a frontal attack, see if you can't make your point by simply reality testing for him.

The second area in which you can try to work things out to your mutual benefit is rather more delicate. Men sometimes have irrational feelings about the house as well, and some of them may have similar conflicts that are brought to the fore by your way of playing your role as housewife. It's certainly obvious that a man can be just as hostile in complaining about a dirty bathtub as his wife was in not cleaning it. More or less. If the house is a source of contention and tension, you have to try to get it back into its place, which should be aided by the reality test you took together as well as reality testing *vis à vis* friends.

One angle you might look at it from, especially if you think part of the problem has to do with the question of role, is that of reassessment. Presumably when you got married you signed an unwritten contract that included clauses specifying certain duties that you and he would fulfill. He probably guaranteed you a certain security in the knowledge that he would work at a job that would bring in sufficient money to support a family. You on your side may well have tacitly agreed to take care of the house and the children. It may be that the contract now needs renegotiating.

You may have taken a job, moved into a larger house, gotten old and feeble, had children—any number of things that may make it more difficult for you to fulfill the conditions. If that's the case, renegotiation can range anywhere from his complete acceptance of your position and the offer of help either from him or from an outside source, to complete refusal to recognize any of your demands or grievances. If the latter proves to be the case, you will have to determine whether capitulation and the denial of your own desires is possible, or whether you're determined to conduct ongoing labor mediations. The most common source of conflict is, I think, over the matter of priorities. A man may object to a woman taking a job because it detracts from his high priority goals for her—to be a wife and mother. The wife may feel that his priorities are off because making a career *is* a high priority goal.

So reaching an accommodation when the problem is one of priorities, rather than one of simple physical needs, is a far-reaching one. In other words, you can get more, but you can't get everything unless you're willing to give up something on your end.

But renegotiating life priorities is such a heavy situation that I direct this mostly to situations where the priorities are similar but there is a lack of awareness on the husband's part of exactly how demanding, ennervating, distressing, or exhausting keeping up a house is.

The most important thing to keep in mind is that you be certain that your demands are reasonably concrete. A discussion that begins with "You don't appreciate me" is doomed to failure. While beginning with a real complaint, along the lines of "I feel pretty pressured having to entertain eighteen people at dinner every Friday, what with the twins on the way next month and two open heart operations to do tomorrow" may jar the complacency of even the most hardened management.

I really feel that I have to stress again that this assumes that you are in basic agreement about your role within the marriage. Because if you're not, it's rubbing salt on the wound, to coin a phrase.

In any case, I can't really advise you about how many of your husband's unreal requests should be included in your Ultimate List. You will have to make your peace with yourself and with him in some probably not too satisfactory fashion. In any case, keep those items that absolutely cannot be scrapped. It goes without saying, of course, that your husband may well have pointed out some things that are quite valid, and these items with whose validity you agree should be retained.

Now, yet again, take pencil and paper and write down everything that didn't get crossed out. That, dear reader, is what you should be doing, your Ultimate List.

Women's Lib aside, at least for the moment, I think it's likely that in looking over what's left you may find that both you and your husband are relatively reasonable people, and that you've simply lost sight of reality around your house, as have the ladies in the following tragic case histories.

Alice Y.

Alice's husband makes fifty thousand dollars a year as a sock manufacturer. Yesterday Alice spent the entire afternoon darning his socks. Alice's husband expressed annoyance because he had had no clean undershirts in three weeks.

Diagnosis: One might speculate that Alice is expressing hostility toward her husband and saying symbolically that she is just as good as he is since they both do things with socks. On the other hand, maybe she's a foot fetishist and also has four hundred pairs of shoes. Whatever the reason, Alice has lost sight of the priorities around her house and should spend some time reality testing. She will also probably require a good bit of attention to rescheduling her working time for efficiency.

Marcia Q.

Mrs. Q., an attractive doctor in her thirties, told of the time that she had to wash the kitchen floor. Not wanting to, because it was one of her most despised tasks, she arranged all the food in her refrigerator alphabetically. She enjoyed doing it and told herself that she was being a good housewife because she had spent a lot of time working in the house.

Diagnosis: Who knows what fantasies washing the floor stirs up in Marcia Q.'s subconscious. Perhaps she really wants to drown her mother and she's so uptight about it that she has to defend against it, not only by avoiding the threatening task, but also by engaging in the obsessive-compulsive task without particular relevance. Maybe she isn't washing the floor because she feels guilty about having an affair and prefers to feel guilty about having a dirty floor. However. Although Marcia essentially knows the priorities, she chooses frequently to ignore them. In addition to making certain that they're properly established, she'll require a schedule to adhere to. If Marcia really has a great outlet in obsessing, at least she could do it where it would do some good.

Claudia P.

Claudia P., who is thought by her employers to be the most competent account executive at her advertising agency, complains that she doesn't know where to start. Or that she can't get going. The other day she walked into the bathroom, having decided the time had come to shave her legs. Through her head went something like: "Hi, ho, time to shave the old legs. . . . Oh hell, there's a ring around the bathtub and the sink is dirty.

"I really should clean out the medicine chest one of these days. What was it that I read somewhere about making hand lotion out of cucumbers or something like that? If I were a better wife I'd do that. . . . I bet the tile would look much better if I went over it with some kerosene or whatever it is you're supposed to use. Oh God. Look at the toilet bowl, it looks like there's a fungus growing in it. Where did I put the toilet bowl brush? . . . Dammit, why didn't I take the curtains down when I got to the kitchen curtains, maybe I'd remember to shorten them? . . ."

And on and on and on until the energy that was going to be expended on the perfectly commendable job of leg shaving gets at best vitiated in a few swipes at the sink, or at worst Claudia staggers out of the john, legs still hairy, muttering vague promises about tomorrow.

Diagnosis: Maybe Claudia is scared to death of responsibility. She might be in the midst of a real conflict about her role and virtually everything is frightening and undoable. She may have led herself into a setup where failure is inevitable. At any rate, Claudia, while she is aware of reality to the extent that she knows what has to be done, has lost sight of relative importance. Faced with the enormity of the job, she's virtually paralyzed and doesn't know where to start. She does things as they occur to her and seldom follows them through. She is frequently depressed. Claudia has to reality test, and, following that, tackle the horrible job of recognizing her house so that it recedes back into something finite that she can deal with. Finally, she has to adopt a schedule to further whittle down the tremendous mushrooming demands that she has become prey to.

Diane R.

Diane has twin three-year-olds. Every morning after making the beds she picks up the whole house. This takes her half an hour. After lunch, while the children are napping, Diane tidies the house again. This takes another half-hour. Before her husband comes home, while the children are watching "Sesame Street," she tidies the entire house, this time throwing things into drawers and closets without any regard for where they make their customary home. Finally, before she goes to bed, Diane puts things away where they belong and tidies up the whole house again. This takes one hour. By and large, Diane's house is tidy and neat, but there are fingermarks all over her walls, her kitchen floor hasn't been washed in a month, and her laundry room is a disaster area. Diane complains that she can't keep up the house without spending all day at it. Diagnosis: Who could say? Maybe she wants to erase her kids by erasing their traces. At any rate, Diane is

spending a cool two and a half hours on the very high
priority job of keeping the house tidy. However, she's
losing sight of reality by spending a disproportionate
amount of time on one job. In her particular case, she
should be picking up the house only once a day. With
small children, Diane needs a schedule to adhere to
that will permit her to handle all the jobs that require
her attention. She can also most probably benefit from
a good course of instruction in how to perform her
housework efficiently.

Arabella K.

Arabella K., married just three months, spent four
hours polishing her dining room table the other day
after some food and candle wax had congealed on it
after dinner the night before. First she rubbed the spots
with Brillo and Spic and Span. Then, noticing that
those spots had whitened, she touched them up with
brown shoe polish, which she thought she'd read about
somewhere as a cure. Then she rubbed the table with
lemon oil polish, then waxed the entire piece with
butcher's wax. Finally, she spent half an hour on the
telephone trying to get hold of a furniture refinisher
who could repair the table before her in-laws, from
whom she had received the table as a wedding present,
came on Saturday.
Diagnosis: Maybe Arabella is expressing her hostility
toward her in-laws. Maybe she can't accept her role
as a wife. Even assuming she knows her priorities, she's
wasting an inordinate amount of time through sheer
ignorance (or acting ignorant). She needs information
on how to do simple things in simple time.

It's easy to see how Diane can turn into Claudia, if
she spends a few weeks neglecting to put things back
in the right place. Her neat but dirty house could turn

into a messy and dirty house with alarming swiftness. And it's not hard to imagine Arabella turning into Alice in time, as she begins to concentrate on the few things that she knows how to do well. So whomever you identify with in this particular series, make sure you're straight on one thing. The very first step is to reality test and to establish what has to be done around your house. And now, somehow, we're going to find the time to do it in.

IV

The Time of Your Time

Reality Test Number 3

The Time of Her Time

HOW MUCH TIME SHOULD YOU SPEND ANYWAY	
If You Live in	*Daily Work Time Should Be*
A studio apartment	½ hour per day
A one-bedroom apartment	1 hour a day
A two-bedroom apartment	2½ hours a day
A six-room house	3 hours a day
An eight-room house	4 hours a day

Two Caveats: (1) This assumes two reasonably clean living adults in whatever size it is. Add ½ hour for each pre-school child, since children have a way of making you start and stop more often, thus cutting down appreciably on your efficiency. (2) It's hard to put a time value on the number of hours you have to work to keep your house in running order, since there are so many factors impinging on it. However, by checking out a lot of people and applying the latest in time-saving devices, I have devised the above very approximate rule of thumb. I would be less than honest if I did not point out that this is not necessarily the amount of time people actually put in on their houses. It's the amount of time they would have to put in if they wanted them in excellent shape.

Write down the time required to keep house clean and neat, although not spotless, and to do laundry and ironing. Do not include child care and cooking. Figure from above chart.

Write underneath that the approximate time you spend taking care of your house, excluding cooking and child care, and any extra projects.

Now subtract time you spend from time required, or vice versa.

Once you've established some realistic aims, as presumably you have in the last chapter, you have to keep your head from sabotaging you. One way you can do it is to lay out the hours that you spend housekeeping so clearly that there's no room for your hangups to work themselves out in.

WHAT YOUR SCORE MEANS IF YOU PRESENTLY SPEND MORE TIME THAN THE SUGGESTED NUMBER OF HOURS:

And if you ask no more than that the house meet the specified conditions, I do hope you're going to discover that by quitting all that stupid fooling around you're going to save enough time to write the Great American Novel (or the Great American Housekeeping Book, if that's your thing), or, heaven forbid, just enjoy yourself. If you feel very uneasy go back and read section III of chapter II.

The same goes if you're spending about the same amount of time that's been suggested, more or less.

IF YOU'RE SLOGGING ALONG AND NOT SPENDING AS MUCH TIME, IS THERE ANY HOPE FOR YOU?

Well, yes.

I had intended to include some sort of neat quiz on how you spent your time, a sort of glorified time and motion study for frustrated efficiency engineers. But the trouble is, there are too many variables. First of all, I have my priorities but I doubt they're the same as yours. Second, the idea of clocking oneself while going about from kitchen to john seems to add more confusion than it removes. So I've decided to content myself with one simple proof of the efficacy of efficiency.

By now you're probably quaking your clogs, it having been pointed out to you that there are any number of things you're not doing that you should be. You're already putting in more time than you should, seeing no end to it, and wondering if you're going to have to start getting up at 6:00 A.M. instead of your usual agonizing 7:42. Just for fun, do this:

Look at the list you made of things that bother you and/or your husband that aren't getting done right. Take maybe five, jot them down, and jot down next to them the amount of time you think it would take per day to get them in good running condition (for the sake of argument, leave out for now the five hours you'll have to spend getting the stove clean and just put down the five minutes a day it would take you to wipe up the spills in the oven). I know it's not fair, but there's a point to it.

Let's say you come up with something like this:

Refrigerator neat	5 minutes
Bathroom smells funny	30 seconds a day to spray with Lysol
Living room a mess	10 minutes a day to straighten

| Glasses have crud on them | 5 minutes a day to scrape dishes instead of throwing them into dishwasher or one second a day to reset dishwasher to wash dishes twice |

Now write down about five things that are okay around your house and that neither one of you cares much about.

You might come up with something like this:

| Cabinets clean | you spend 10 minutes a day cleaning off the top shelf of your cabinet because your mother used to |
| Laundry dazzling white | you spend at least an hour a week soaking and bleaching and bluing your husband's and son's underwear, which they couldn't care less about as long as it is reasonably clean.* |

So, right off the bat, you're saving time and reality testing and substituting necessary jobs for unnecessary ones.

Let's suppose that I'm totally and horribly wrong and you haven't been doing anything unnecessary and now you've just found out a whole lot more things you have to do and you don't spend anywhere near that much time on your house and you'd kill yourself if you had to. Don't give up here, because it's extremely probable that corners can be cut where you didn't even know there were corners. It may very well be that you there in your six-room house think that three hours a

---

* In addition to which you are committing mass homicide on scads of fish, who are dying from the pollutants you're putting in the water, and playing into the hands of the manufacturers by cooperating in the planned obsolescence of perfectly good underwear which you are destroying long before its natural life would run out.

day is an intolerable and unreasonable amount of time for any thinking woman to spend on cleaning a house. Since it happens that I thoroughly agree with you, I am delighted to propose the Psychiatrist's Wife's Rule for How to Get Away with Less Work if You're Willing to Take the Consequences.

EASE, ELEGANCE, AND ECONOMY

It was pointed out to me by one of my more stable friends that the reason that she and I and everyone we know live in a state of relative mess and suffer the agonies of the damned over our inability to be superwomen is that we are attempting to take on a mutually exclusive set of circumstances.

It goes like this. The three elements you're dealing with in keeping your house are:

> Ease
> Elegance
> Economy

You can never have all three at the same time.

You can have ease and elegance without economy: Hire a full-time maid.

You can have elegance and economy without ease: Be your own full-time maid.

You can have ease and economy without elegance: Do your house over in formica, linoleum, and contact paper. (That wonderful summer cottage that takes five minutes a day to keep clean is a perfect example of ease and economy.)

The question of where you compromise should be settled by referring to your Ultimate List from the last chapter. If it's apparent that in reality an antiseptically clean house is not vital to your mental health, leave out things like sweeping out the fireplace, washing the windows, or vacuuming the upholstery, when you figure out the time it takes you to clean a room. And DON'T

FEEL GUILTY about it, because you should have convinced yourself that it doesn't really matter. Hopefully, there will come a day when the house is so organized that you'll be able to spend some of your time cleaning it. On the rather odd chance that your particular thing is dirt, forget about any time organizing and get right at that filthy oven.

So, keeping in mind the general number of hours you're willing to spend, you're ready to examine the weighty question of

Why a Schedule?

Think back to the case histories illustrating faulty reality testing. In all the cases considered in our scientific study, we prescribed a schedule as part of the cure. Let's consider what the possible advantages of a schedule would be to you:

1. It would make the work finite, thereby cutting down on disorganization, duplication, substitution of unnecessary jobs for necessary ones, or the wages of displacement.

2. It would cut most of the guilt that you feel at not getting to things because you would know that you were eventually going to get to them. Consider how Claudia would have felt when she entered the bathroom to shave her legs had she known that Tuesday was her day for giving the bathroom a general cleaning, next Wednesday the time for bathroom repairs, when she'd get to the curtains, and there was a day planned late in the month that included her semi-annual medicine chest cleanup.

You have got to fool your unconscious, which is working against you all the time, throwing you random thoughts chock full of unpleasant fantasies that you have to exorcise. Because I don't trust anybody's subconscious to mind its own business when you're cleaning, I recommend constructing a structured plan to keep you on the path to virtue.

3. It would give you yet another wonderful obsessive-compulsive thing to do. A good schedule should take at least two hours to make, not even counting drawing in things in two different colors.

4. It would redirect those nice obsessive-compulsive impulses to some area where they'd have good effect.

5. Again, it imposes artificial order on the house and, if you're affected by your house, on you.

MAKING A SCHEDULE

By now you should have a better idea of the priorities in your home. The objective now is to fit the jobs into a schedule that you can realistically follow. Beware, beware of falling victim to built-in failure—taking on so much that Nobody could possibly do it, which gives you a wonderful rationalization for why you can't. So don't plan, at least for now, on spending more time than you are presently.

By and large, jobs divide themselves into three, or possibly four, categories.

One caveat. There is no way that I can even approximate how long it would take you to, say, clean a living room. If you want to judge a time, flip to Chapter X on how to clean rooms for some idea of what's involved. You may be able to make a stab.

DAILY JOBS

The only job that has to be considered a daily one is a general once over tidying of the house, which should take from fifteen minutes to an hour, depending on the size of your home. It's possible that your child has a fantastic dust allergy and the dog has to be vacuumed daily, or maybe your husband finds the absence of a fresh towel in the bathroom a threat to his machismo. In any case, your daily jobs should be relatively few. Write them down.

WEEKLY JOBS

A friend of mine, who lives alone and works for an airline, spends ten days out of every thirty away from her house. She assures me that giving her bedroom an hour's worth of work once a month and her living room and kitchen the same keeps everything completely shipshape. On the other hand, another friend of mine, who used to work for an airline until she married a pilot with visions of operating a family airline, and now has five children under six, tells me that it's necessary to clear out the underbrush in the children's rooms twice a week or she has difficulty finding the youngest one. But if your situation is anywhere near normal, you'd probably be safe in figuring on a cleaning of each room in the house once a week and laundry and marketing are two other probable weekly jobs. Whatever they are, write them down.

MONTHLY JOBS

Monthly jobs have a way of being put off until they turn into semi-annual horrors, unless you have a schedule and stick to it. Take something like defrosting the freezer or mucking out the stove. Ideally, it should probably be done once a month. But what is ideal in this world of ours? One of the benefits of a schedule is to avoid turning simple, frequent jobs into ghastly infrequent ones. It's possible that you're the sort of person who can cope with a freezer defrosting, a stove cleaning, and a wall washing every spring, but you should give some consideration to the possibility that doing jobs with greater frequency might save you not only time in the long run, but also avoid those horrible days when the last lone ice cube tray refuses to be squeezed back into the freezer. I've listed monthly jobs as I see them, under the section on how to clean rooms. However, it's conceivable that you have other ideas. If so, do it your way.

SEASONAL JOBS

Like monthly jobs, only they take a little longer before they catch up with you. Washing your curtains is a seasonal job, or it should be. Turning a rug once a year so that it gets even wear is another one. Again, refer to the section on how to clean rooms.

How to Draw Up a Schedule

Reproduce on a big piece of paper the chart on page 62.

Now the idea is essentially to go around taking one from column A, one from column B, and so on.

First, list your daily jobs in every day's space.

Second, divide your weekly jobs, which hopefully shouldn't number more than seven, zipping one into each day under the daily jobs.

Third, spread around your monthly and seasonal jobs, trying to keep from lumping them together in one week. If it's a monthly kitchen job, add it on underneath the weekly kitchen cleaning. If it's a seasonal living room job, put it under living room weekly cleaning.

In the interest of compulsiveness, which is my own thing, I am appending a schedule, to give you an idea of what I mean. This is for Ann, who is recently married and lives in a 3½-room apartment (living room, bedroom, and kitchen—the ½ is thrown in presumably because there is a coat closet). Ann works during the day, as does her husband. While Ann calls for and generally gets help from her husband when there's a red alert, like unexpected guests, she's not yet quite liberated enough to divide the tasks evenly. Her schedule looks about like the chart on page 63.

Apparently Ann should have to average no more than an hour's work a day, in addition to the time it takes her to make dinner. But, if Ann didn't want to spare the hour she could cut down by harking back to ease, efficiency, and elegance. A maid for Ann, half a day a week, would cut her daily work down to a half hour, if that.

If living by schedule seems somewhat rigid to you, you're perfectly right. It's supposed to be pretty rigid. After all, if you want to keep housework from becoming infinite, you have to structure it. Try to think of it like a diet. If you want to get the old pounds off, you have to stick to some pretty rigid rules about what to eat. And as all the diet books are fond of saying, the whole object is to reeducate your body in new ways of eating. It's the same way with cleaning your house. Nobody expects you to like it, but if you stick to your plan, you should emerge a Better Person For It. WARNING: DO NOT embark on a diet simultaneously with starting a new household regime.

On the other hand, remember that a starvation diet is usually doomed to failure. Don't, at least to begin with, attempt to put in more hours than you're presently working.

The major premise of the schedule, remember, is that, if housework becomes finite, it becomes less infinitely impossible to tackle. If it becomes regimented, so that each day has its own necessities, then every day should care for itself. And the harder it will be to act irrelevantly and destructively.

Monday	Tuesday	Wednesday	Thursday	Friday	Saturday	Sunday

Three Rooms
(L.R., B.R., Kitchen + Bath)

Average Time
9 1/4 Hours /week
1 1/4 - 1 1/2 Hours /day

General - 1/4 Kitchen weekly - 1/2 Kitchen monthly - 1/2 (defrost) 1 1/4	General - 1/4 Livingroom weekly - 1/2 Livingroom monthly - 1/2 (vacuum rugs) Livingroom seasonal - 1 (clean, wax furn.) 2 1/4	General - 1/4 Bedroom weekly - 1/2 Bedroom monthly - 1/2 (brush curtains, make repairs) 1 1/4	General - 1/4 Marketing - 1 1 1/4	General - 1/4 Bathroom weekly - 1/2 Bathroom monthly - 1/2 (clean tiles) 1 1/4	General - 1/4 Laundry - 1/2 3/4	General - 1/4 D.O. - 1/2 3/4
General - 1/4 Kitchen weekly - 1/2 Kitchen monthly - 1/2 (stove) 1 1/4	General - 1/4 Livingroom weekly - 1/2 Livingroom monthly - 1/2 (tidy shelves, magazines) 1 1/4	General - 1/4 Bedroom weekly - 1/2 Bedroom monthly - 1/2 (tidy night tables + 1 dresser) Bedroom seasonal - 3/4 (clean floors) 2	General - 1/4 Marketing - 1 1 1/4	General - 1/4 Bathroom weekly - 1/2 Bathroom monthly - 1/2 (wash window inside) 1 1/4	General - 1/4 Laundry - 1/2 Ironing - 1 1 3/4	General - 1/4 D.O. - 1/2 3/4
General - 1/4 Kitchen weekly - 1/2 Kitchen monthly - 1/2 (1 cabinet, polish silver) 1 1/4	General - 1/4 Livingroom weekly - 1/2 Livingroom monthly - 1/2 (repairs) 1 1/4	General - 1/4 Bedroom weekly - 1/2 Bedroom monthly - 1/4 (turn mattress) 1	General - 1/4 Marketing - 1 1 1/4	General - 1/4 Bathroom weekly - 1/2 Bathroom monthly - 1/4 (tidy med. chest) Bathroom seasonal - 1/4 (hamper) 1 1/4	General - 1/4 Laundry - 1/2 Ironing - 1 1 3/4	General - 1/4 D.O. - 1/2 3/4
General - 1/4 Kitchen weekly - 1/2 Kitchen monthly - 3/4 (wash insides windows, repairs) 1 1/2	General - 1/4 Livingroom weekly - 1/2 Livingroom monthly - 1/2 (wash insides windows) 1 1/4	General - 1/4 Bedroom weekly - 1/2 Bedroom monthly - 1/2 (wash insides windows) 1 1/4	General - 1/4 Marketing - 1 1 1/4	General - 1/4 Bathroom weekly - 1/2 Bathroom monthly - 1/4 (repairs) 1	General - 1/4 Laundry - 1/2 Mending - 1 1 3/4	General - 1/4 D.O. - 1/2 3/4

What If You Get Sick Or Something Horrible Like That?

Well, what if you go off a diet? You go back double in starving yourself the next day. If you do get sick, or otherwise can't cope, try to double up when you feel better.

What If You Have Cleaning Help?

Then it should follow, as the cigarette burns on the rug after a party, that you'll be better able to separate out those jobs which are the ones you hate the most and assign them to the person who helps you clean. Ditto, if you have other help, like a teenage daughter. Now, instead of bitching at her to keep her room clean or for God's sake help you around the house for a change, you and she can agree on an amount of time that she should give to housekeeping and you can parcel out the jobs accordingly.

What If You're a Liberated Woman?

Several possibilities are open to you. The two of you can work alternate days. Or you can split the hours in half. Or you can turn it all over to him since it really takes so little time.

What About All the Things We Didn't Mention Like Preparing Dinner Parties and Baking Cookies?

Oh come on. Obviously some days you're going to have to slave away. If you have to put in an extra three hours because Guess Who is coming to dinner, then have the motherwit to shove the day's work to another day, or break it up over the course of the week. If you feel that baking chocolate chip cookies once a week is essential to your children's moral development, then make room for it in the schedule. Remember to set realistic attainable goals.

What If Everything Is a Mess and It's Futile to Even Think About Setting Up a Schedule, When You Don't Even Know What Room to Shovel Out First?

If that's the case, and it may well be, you'll have to make up your first month's schedule rather differently. Go very light on weekly cleaning. Tidy the house once a day and concentrate on repair jobs, reorganization of the rooms, and equipment. Having done so for a month, your house will hardly be appreciably dirtier than it is now, and you'll be ready to begin a real schedule with as few extra jobs as possible. If you can possibly afford it, this is the time to hire a maid or a cleaning service to get the rooms once and for all clean after you have them reorganized. If you can't, after you've finished your reorganization, get started on thorough cleaning the rooms one by one. But try to make *some* sort of a schedule, even if it still allows for a certain amount of chaos. It will be a help anyway.

What If You're Really Tired and It Doesn't Work?

If keeping up with a schedule becomes too difficult, let the major cleaning jobs languish and keep at the organizational or occasional jobs. In other words, your priorities should be:

1. Make *some* kind of schedule and try to keep as close as you can to it, because it will cut the whole of housekeeping down to more manageable size.

2. Concentrate on the *real* needs, because they are, strangely enough, the most important.

3. Attempt to create some order within your house, since that should help to increase order all around, including in your head.

4. Actually get things undirty.

If you cut back and you still can't do it by a schedule (maybe the idea of knowing what you're doing is threatening because it stirs up the sludge in your subconscious) you might as well give up, count your blessings, and flip through the back of the book to see if you can find little ways to save time when you're motivated to clean. You could also get analyzed to find out why you can't work under a schedule, but all in all it's probably cheaper to hire a maid once a week.*

A Few Ground Rules

The more clever reader may have noticed that there is perhaps a benign neglect of one or two areas. For instance, cooking. Or cleaning up after you cook. Or doing laundry. Or what's the most unhassled way of getting this all done.

It's almost as impossible as figuring out how long it would take your average everyday housewife to clean a living room (is it 10 by 10 or 40 by 30; do you collect and display old Roman collar bones that must be dusted daily?). Take cooking, for instance. There are a fantastic number of time-saving devices you can use. (Most of which I am hoarding for my cookbook.) For instance:

You can fill your sink with soapy water as you begin to cook and throw in bowls, spoons, and whatnots as soon as you finish using them.

You can, especially if you have a small family, cook double and trade off with a friend. (You thought I was

---

* If you figure analysis at $40 an hour, four times a week for four years, it amounts to about $30,000. That means roughly that you could get a cleaning woman to clean your house at $15 a day once a week for the next forty years. Of course that is a horrible way to look at the cost of psychoanalysis, but it is quite sound mathematically. I have always thought that a good way to decide whether or not you needed to be shrunk was to think about whether you had any problems that couldn't be solved by spending $7,500 a year on whatever you felt like (two mink coats, or seventy-five $100 dresses, or five trips to Europe) until somebody pointed out to me that nobody ever blew $7,500 a year without getting to feel so guilty they'd need to be analyzed out of it.

going to say freeze half for another meal. You can, of course, do this, but it seldom works out somehow. What usually happens is that it gets buried in the freezer and when you're defrosting two months later you decide it's gone bad or you didn't like the way it tasted the first time, anyway.)

You can take out all your ingredients, assemble them on the counter, and put them away right after you use them one by one.

However, none of these helpful hints is particularly helpful when it comes to actually figuring out when to do things. Take, for instance, the worst times of the day:

GETTING UP IN THE MORNING

Getting up in the morning is a dreadful job in itself. That you should be saddled with the additional horror of actually feeding people is grotesque. However, if you have to, you can achieve some success with the following:

1. Set the table the night before (perhaps as you unload the dishwasher or drainboard).

2. Throw away the rulebooks about serving hearty breakfasts, and serve dry cereal, orange juice, and milk or coffee (how many eggs actually get eaten around your house?).

Except for the exceptional case (those women who wake up all glowing) nothing should be attempted at breakfast time other than breakfast. If you work and you find getting yourself and sundry out of the house ranges from difficult to impossible, try doing as much as you can the night before (do the kitchen things while you're cleaning up after dinner).

1. Set the table
2. Make orange juice
3. Put coffee in coffee pot

4. Write any messages to your sitter, housekeeper, or whatever

5. Lay out your clothes (all of them, even your jewelry)

6. Lay out kid's clothes, if any (kids, that is)

7. Put by the front door whatever you and/or your husband and/or your child/children need to take along in the morning.

In other words, realize that the human body generally functions at less than peak capacity in the morning, and the less strain you put on it, the longer you will probably live.

DOING THE DIRTY WORK

Here you just have to judge when you're best equipped to tackle the odious job. Some women like to get at it first thing; others prefer to put it off as long as humanly possible and serve some really disastrous meals that way because they wax the kitchen floor and then can't get back to the oven to baste the chicken.

If you work, I think I have to recommend the briefest of cleaning before you take off, since nothing attenuates a rotten feeling at 5:30 like dishes on the table and unmade beds. Some variation of the Elizabeth Taylor Cleanup (see Chapter X) is probably a good idea. I also understand that there are some women who get up at 5:00 A.M. to get their chores done before the family arises. I don't know any personally (although I have my suspicion about one or two), but it makes me shudder. However, on one or two occasions I've found myself awake ten minutes or so before everybody else and I've sat down and read the paper and had a cup of coffee, and I must say it's a positively joyous feeling to feel halfway friendly toward children when they wake up. So you could think about some variations on that. If you like getting it all over with early, and you're home much of the day, make sure that you stick to your guns and do only what you have to, or what you've scheduled yourself to do.

Try not to do anything that's not in your schedule. If you're seized with a mad desire to get the rings off the coffee table today instead of tomorrow, make sure you change the jobs around in your head, if not on paper. This avoids going off your housekeeping diet, as it were. It may help to differentiate between obsessive-compulsive jobs and non-obsessive-compulsive jobs, because sometimes you may feel you need to do an obsessive-compulsive job and you will go off your rocker if you just go and sweep out the bedroom. If that's one of your problems, scatter them around liberally. Just make sure you do something that's supposed to be done, instead of whipping up something totally irrelevant.

On the other hand, if you opt to do your work late in the day, make sure you're convinced that you really will, or else you'll spend the entire day feeling guilty about not doing it.

Don't break up the work into intervals of less than a half an hour. Stopping and starting generally cuts your efficiency drastically. Try to do all your work in one part of the day. Most of us find it hard to start. Starting three times a day is three times harder than starting once.

Never do a job more than once, like Diane, like taking a swipe at the table and then doing it thoroughly two hours later.

Do the hard things first. I don't know why this is, but if you have four walls to wash and you pick out the one you really loathe the most and do it first, the whole thing seems a lot more bearable. You can apply this to which chair to vacuum first, or which table to dust first, or which spilled bottle of milk to cry over first.

If you have a great deal of trouble getting started, there are one or two things I can think of that might con you into actually getting off your bottom. One is to set a kitchen timer and to promise yourself to move as soon as it rings. The other is to promise yourself some reward after you've completed the dreadful task. What your reward is depends on what turns you on.

Try doing two things at once, like:

folding laundry while you're talking on the phone to your mother,

polishing silver while you're watching television,

planning menus while you're making love (As you can see, this method has a tendency to get out of hand. I have a friend who has gotten into such bad shape that she's unable to go to the opera without taking along her mending. So use this method in moderation.)

DINNER TIME

Although it's generally true that you're more wide awake at dinner time than you are at breakfast, you probably also are more tired. In fact there may well be nights when you'd like to nibble on a leaf of lettuce, but your husband considers any dinner under four courses a meager, wretched offering, causing resentment to well up over the pot of boeuf en daube. If you don't work, but you consistently find the thought of cooking too much to bear, you might consider how the rule of ease, elegance, and economy relates to cooking:

You can have ease and elegance without economy: Hire a cook, or have all your meals catered, or serve filet mignon every night.

You can have economy and ease without elegance: Serve hamburgers every night and switch to hot dogs on Sunday.

You can have economy and elegance without ease: Spend three hours before dinner baking your own bread, concocting your own sauces, and making a superb steak out of Sunday's hot dogs.

Somewhere, there's a compromise, and hopefully

this side of the rainbow. Go back to Chapter II and find out why you're so hung up on cooking. Put Julia on the top shelf for a month and use Peg Bracken's *I Hate to Cook Book*. See if anybody cares. And if you don't work and you think you've got it rough when dinner time rolls around, cast a thought to your sisters who toil outside the home and return, most usually, to chaos.

SOME RANDOM BUT NEVERTHE-LESS IMPORTANT THOUGHTS FOR WOMEN WHO WORK

If you'll recall what we said in the second chapter about working and roles, you'll see that this can be applied to scheduling. A constant switching back and forth between, say, lawyer and mother takes a certain resilience and the more you can separate things, the less likely you are to go all confused. I never realized, for instance, the validity of the father who comes home from the office and sinks slowly into the newspaper, until I became a working mother. There has to be some transition, and the more gently transition can be made, the better things generally will go. I think this applies most usually to women who both work and have children; most husbands can usually be put off with a muttered, "Hard day at the office." Children, unfortunately, cannot, especially because mothers who work suffer from some degree of guilt and feel that they should be with their kids as much as they can when they're home. Transition, unfortunately, takes time, and the first place to look is how you can make an extra ten minutes or half an hour. To make the flow from work to home less abrupt you could, for instance:

take a shorter lunch and leave fifteen minutes early,
take a taxi instead of a bus,
have your sitter stay a little longer.

All of these assume that you'd actually take the fifteen minutes to sit down with a mystery or do your needle-point or do whatever it is that you do that helps you relax. Because if you don't you're just taking fifteen minutes away from work and adding fifteen minutes on to the children. How you do it is up to you; older children will often respond to a request for fifteen minutes of peace and quiet before you turn on to them. It varies with littler ones. One woman I know stops in at a neighbor's for ten minutes, another one lets herself in quietly by the back door and sneaks upstairs while her kids are watching "Sesame Street" and appears somewhat more smoothed out when "Mr. Rogers" comes on.

If finding a time slot for transition isn't possible, the next best thing is to have as little as possible planned for the first hour or half-hour that you come home. A woman who comes in at 5:30 and, before 7:30 has to feed and bathe the children, make martinis, change her clothes, make dinner for her husband, tidy up the house, and fold the laundry, is not only not going to feel up to writing the Great American Novel after dinner, she is unlikely to want to do anything other than sit for thirty minutes in a dark closet with her knees pulled up to her chin. Simplify. Can the sitter feed and bathe the kids? A lot of mothers who work really want to have the family all together at dinner time, but if you came home to children already fed and bathed, and if you and your husband had dinner alone after the kids went to bed, you might have a free hour in which to just dig your children. As well as a quiet dinner time in which to dig your husband.

If your sitter (assuming your kids are little and you have one) can't be persuaded to spend ten minutes before you come home tidying up the grosser signs of chaos, something's wrong. Go read the chapter on maids. If your children are large enough to let them-selves in after school, they should be given the distinct impression that if you walk into pandemonium, there's an awfully good chance you might walk right back out again.

I think I'd go as far as to say that, if you work and you have a family, you should move heaven and earth, and your husband and your savings account, to employ enough cleaning help so you can be relieved of at least one segment of your crowded life. If that's not possible, the next best thing is to delegate some of the tasks to your husband and/or your children. If that's not possible (have you really tried?) you should consider that women who work and raise families often suffer from a superwoman complex, which is to say that they feel that they can and/or should do a superb job of working and housewifing. Not terribly many can, and if you can't or don't want to quit your job, you'll either have to continue to live in a state of harassment (assuming that you are) or have to compromise with your standards (is it really a sin to serve hollandaise out of a jar instead of made by your own two work-gnarled hands? Couldn't you have friends in for just drinks instead of dinner? Is it really out of the question to resort to Chinese take-out food some of the time? Will your children stop loving you if you don't send a batch of chocolate chip cookies to school every week? Will your husband lose his job if his undershirts are not whiter than white?) There are always priorities. The point is to establish them realistically and, when you have to cut something out, to make sure it's the least important.

In any case, if you work, and have a family and have the major responsibility for getting rid of dirt, try to plan it in chunks and try to avoid a half-cleanup, half-playing with your kids situation. It seems to me better to plant them in front of the tube Saturday morning (really, everybody does, you oughtn't to feel so guilty) and get it done then, and have the rest of the day free, than to spend the whole day cutting in and out on playing Candyland so you can go back to cleaning out the closets.

I see we have gotten rather far from dinner time and into the dark night of the soul. Try to remember that if your priorities are valid, any guilt you heap on yourself is neurotic, masochistic, ulcer-producing, and altogether no good.

V

Children

OR,
HOW TO AVOID THE BATTERED MOTHER SYNDROME

Although this is not intended to be a book about sex, there is one point that seems relevant. As of this writing, there is as yet no known means as effective as sexual intercourse for producing those little bundles of incipient neurosis that turn the capable young working wife's charming and well-kept three-room pad into a six or eight rooms of total, mind-boggling horror.

The vicious circle that often starts after the birth of a baby has very little to do with the baby itself. After all, it's not so much a matter of what a baby under six months can do as what he can't. He can't affect your house, by himself, unless you're partial to sitting him on the sofa after he's had his bottle and before he's had his burp. (And once you've turned your sofa cushions once, there is no place else to go.) So it's not that the change which you may have noticed, or maybe will notice, is caused by the little thing. The change comes from a variety of causes.

1. You may be tired after you've had a baby.

If you're tired, and if you haven't laid in very much help, it's awfully easy for the house to get away from you. (It may have had a head start in the days or week you were in the hospital when your husband made do without you.) The more there is to do, the harder it is to get started. The longer you wait to get started, the more there is to do.

2. With a baby in the house, and even if it's a good one, there's more to do—sterilizing diapers, folding them, bottles, and what not.

3. If you've quit work to stay home with a baby, you're going to be in the house a lot more than you're used to. The more you stay in a house, the more you'll notice the things you should do that you never thought of doing before when you were out of it most of the day.

4. If you've quit work, the loss of income may have forced you to give up cleaning help, making your load that much greater.

5. *Not everyone takes to motherhood.* In fact a sizable number of women feel angry, resentful, as though they've been conned, or forced into a job (or a role) that they dislike. After awhile—it may be days, weeks, or months (sometimes, but not too usually, it's never)—the ball starts to roll, as it were, again, but, for the duration, the anger a new mother feels toward the poor sweet defenseless baby and which she finds virtually impossible to direct toward him, usually makes itself felt toward herself. She may become depressed and unable to do anything around the house. Or it may be displaced onto her husband (she may consciously or unconsciously blame him for causing her unhappiness). Since she associates her child so closely with her house, particularly if she has never stayed home before to such an extent, she may also take her anger out on her house, either in neglect or, not infrequently, by breaking things. If you're aware enough of your own feelings to see this developing inside your

head, there are several possible courses open to you, other than killing yourself, your husband, or the baby, or all three:

You can get the hell out of the house, either back to work full-time or part-time, or back to school, or just for pleasure.

You can lighten your load as much as is financially possible by hiring someone to clean your house and/or take care of your baby.

You can try to talk out your feelings with your husband or, if that's not possible, with a friend who has, you suspect, had similar feelings.

If you're still feeling this way after, say, six months, and it shows no sign of abating, you should take definite steps to either change your life style in one of the first two ways or, if there's no one close to you to speak to, or if you meet with too much hostility when you express your own feelings, you ought to give some thought to talking with an outside, objective source—your family doctor, your clergyman or even, what the hell, a shrink. After all, if your functioning has fallen off considerably, you ought to think about fixing it up, just as you'd think about fixing up your stomach if you had cramps every day for three hours.

I'm going on at such length about kids for several reasons. But I think it could be summed up by saying that in one way or another kids contribute to disorder and contribute their share of conflicts—some of which work themselves out on the house. It would stand to reason, wouldn't it, that if there were some way to make the whole kid thing less of a bother, it might help around the rest of the house.

Assuming you've gotten over the trauma of becoming a mother, or you never had any trauma, or you've never felt more capable of housekeeping in your whole life, there are still a number of pragmatic things you can do to make life a little bit easier when the baby stops being a virtual vegetable and discovers creeping and crawling as a way out of that boring blue blanket.

How to Babyproof Your House

First, get down on your hands and knees and crawl around the living room. Do this preferably when you are alone, or maybe you could try doing it with your husband which might be interesting if you don't do it too close to the eleven o'clock feeding. There are all manner of fascinating things at this level—light cords which, you may notice if you're relatively sober, are attached to lamps. If you are an incorrigible empiricist, you can try tugging at one to see what will happen. Most of these cords can either be tacked down or put behind furniture by using extension cords. You should be able to buy in any hardware store a little thing-amabob to stick in open sockets. Although no kid I've ever known has ever shown the slightest interest in electric outlets, I have heard that some children think it's more fun than sampling rat poison to stick a diaper pin in the little bitty hole. If you can't find these things, you can tape over the hole with adhesive tape or with a Band Aid. This is rather second best, since it's inevitable that you're going to use some of the sockets some of the time and it's easier to stick the things in again than to hunt up a new piece of adhesive. Keep some extras around.

Next, note objects on low and especially shaky tables. You may handle this in two ways:

1. Say goodbye to everything breakable, or put it on the mantel or someplace out of reach. This is known in the trade as taking the course of least resistance. It does, however, make for a depressingly dull living room. It also sets a precedent for determining who exactly is controlling the way you live in your house. So think a little bit about:

2. Removing the most valuable or breakable objects

and saying no to the child when he touches the ones that remain. A child at about a year will often (note, I did not say always, so refrain from sending me bills for replacing Ming vases) respond to being led around the room and being told in a firm but friendly voice* that "This vase is a no-no because Mommy and Daddy love it and they don't want it to get hurt." Do remember that it's a good idea to have some semi no-no's, that is, things you don't let the baby touch usually, but when you're on a long distance call with your old college roommate and the kid is bugging you, you let him play with it. (I *know* this isn't consistent and I know how important it's supposed to be to be consistent, but anyone who's ever lived with a child for more than two days and can consistently be consistent must either be a child psychiatrist or catatonic.)

Now, though you swore you never would, is the time to give serious thought to slipcovers. Not plastic. Just nice cotton or whatever slipcovers. Remember, however, that most people don't remember to take the slipcovers off for guests. So the slipcovers get all ratty looking, which is not any better than having ratty looking upholstery, and in five years when you remove the slipcovers in an orgy of expectation, you discover that you hate the upholstery, or that half the stains have come through. But you can clean slipcovers pretty easily. You can also have upholstery cleaned, only not as easily or cheaply. And watch out for velvet—water and milk spots often will not come out—not even if cleaned professionally. Also, I tend to think that Scotchgard is useless, except on heavy cottons and weaves which bear up pretty well except under cranberry juice. (If you get your kid hooked on apple juice in his bottle, rather than milk or orange juice, you'll have fewer ugly stains. Avoid grape juice altogether.)

---

* Try it, and when you've perfected it, tape record it, because I have never been able to master the trick.

You can try to institute a rule by which one of my friends has managed to keep a relatively decent living room after five years of two kids. There is an absolute prohibition, punishable by death and disfigurement, against eating or drinking (by children) in the living room. And try to keep the living room off limits when you're going through toilet training and letting the kid run around without diapers. All right, I just said try.

One other thing about upholstery. Designate a good side and a bad side to all turnable cushions. But remember, a sloppy grown-up friend can ruin your good side just as easily as a kid can.

If it happens that you're about to repaint your house, you might consider doing all your woodwork in flat black paint or some equally depressing dark color. Otherwise, live with it. You can try to steer kids to doorknobs, and you can try to get them to wash up surgically as soon as they enter the house. You can also try to fit an elephant on the head of a pin.

I learned something the other day that may well be the single most valuable tip in the book. It's remarkable that I haven't read it in any housekeeping book, but there you are. If you want to avoid having your mahogany tables looking like the fingerprint file of Scotland Yard, DON'T USE SO MUCH WAX or polish. (For how-to, read the chapter on furniture.) Better yet, if you have a choice, don't buy furniture with a high gloss. Teak, walnut, and woods with an oil finish show up with few if any fingerprints.

If you have white wall-to-wall carpeting, you'd better put a padlock on the door and electrify all entrances. If you have a choice of finish for uncovered wood floors, if you somehow can't bring yourself to put linoleum in the living room, have the floors finished with a penetrating oil stain (read the section on floors). Shellacked floors will water spot as will those that are Fabuloned or varnished. Polyurethaned floors will scratch. A floor with a light dull finish will show up far less dirt and garbage than a dark shiny one.

You are now, thank God, out of the living room. Except to go back in to say one more thing. If you live in a three-room apartment, it would be cruel and unnatural to expect your kid to keep out of the living room. On the other hand, if there's plenty of play space available, you may consider making a rule along the lines of: "You're welcome in the living room to sit and talk, but this is a sitting and talking room and not one where you bring your toys or your food." No child under five can bear sitting still for more than five minutes, and after they're five the destruction factor is considerably cut.

As for bedroom, dining room, and study or den, the rules are basically the same and the rules you make for your children will have to be your own. Do try to:

1. Arrange your books so that the old science fiction paperbacks are on the bottom shelf and the signed first edition Freud is up higher. Also, keep in mind that crawlers have a way of learning to walk, and children, by and large, do get taller with time. So keep after it. You can try packing in your books really tight, but

a) most babies, by dint of their superhuman effort, can pry them out and

b) playing with crummy old paperbacks can be loads of fun for the baby, no sacrifice to you, and how do you know he won't be a writer when he grows up?

2. Find *some* way to get your record player out of reach. It's awfully difficult to train a kid to keep away from something so unbelievably fascinating. (The lights! The sound! The Way It Moves!) This is a situation where the course of least resistance is the better part of valor. Or something like that. The same thing goes for your records. Get them out of the way if you possibly can, and if not, pack them in as tightly as you can and pray.

If you have any storage cabinets, secure them with a

rubber band, or a dog leash thing or, in extremis, a padlock. Depending upon the motor ability of your kid, by the time he's learned to open them all he couldn't care less about what's inside.

If you have cabinets that can't be locked or desk drawers that are easy to open, root through them for your stationery from Cartier's your complete set of magic markers, your cameras and film. Surely there must be someplace else.

The Bathroom

Most children don't have the ability to get themselves up for a look in the medicine chest until they're old enough to know that all that stuff in there is what the wicked queen used for Snow White's apple. However, better safe than stuck one afternoon with a child who's gaily waving an empty iodine bottle at you. You probably should get the more virulent stuff out of the medicine chest and onto the top shelf of a closet. It's a good idea to take out the lock on the bathroom door and thus avoid having to call the fire department. You can replace it with a hook and eye far up if you value your privacy.

On the subject of poisons, your area may have a poison control center which is handy for when your two-year-old samples your gourmet roach trap. As it happened, mine did, and I called the poison control center and they told me, after they'd sent someone over with a hypodermic to stop my hysterics, that traps, while not exactly the nutritional equivalent of Flintstones Vitamins, were virtually harmless nowadays unless consumed by the handful. So, if it's a nibble that your kid takes, and if he is not apparently frothing at the mouth, you might call poison control. On the other hand, if you're panicked, or if the child is turning green and you can't remember if you're supposed to induce vomiting or turn him upside down and shake hard, and your eyes are too misted over to read the fine print on poisons in Dr. Spock, just scoop up the kid and get him to the nearest doctor or hospital emergency room.

The bathtub isn't too much of a problem—not too many kids fall in, although I once found one happily playing with bath toys in a dry bathtub. Why not anyway? If you want to avoid scalding your kid on a hot hot water faucet, get into the habit of running hot water first, then cooling it with cold—this leaves cold water in the pipes, so if he turns on the hot in playful abandon when you've got your back turned, it will be a minute before scalding hot water comes gushing out. Also, on the odd chance that you enjoy listening to the radio in the bathroom, remove it, because if any plugged-in electrical appliance gets pulled into the tub, you have just invented the electric bathtub and you will have to start all over again with a new child.

Try to remember to leave the toilet closed. While water play is recommended by many preschool educators as being desirable, when it takes place in Mommy's bathroom right before a dinner party when big brother forgot to flush again, it couldn't matter if it raised baby's I.Q. by 40 points.

With toilet tissue, you can take one of three routes:

1. Strong no-no's. (Basically, you must remember that little kids are really stupid. Even if they can count to ten by the time they're fifteen months old, they don't learn to abstract until much later. That means that if you give a kid a roll of paper towels as a toy and make approving clucking noises, he will find it hard to understand why you have a fit when you find him unrolling the toilet paper.)

2. Take the toilet tissue and put it out of reach, carefully remembering to keep it within reach of those who need it or

3. Bear with the tissue paper tearing for a month or so. They get bored with it, you will have avoided count-

less fights, and the depressing sight of bare toilet tissue on the bathroom shelf.

I will now give you, gratis, one of my rules for child rearing, which I will expound on unmercifully in my forthcoming (1998) book, *The Psychiatrist's Wife's Guide to Child Rearing* or *How to Keep Your Head Without Bashing In Anybody Else's*. Be careful with your "no's." Make sure you care. It was a revelation to me when I realized that there was absolutely no reason why my son couldn't ride his tricycle in the house. When I was little there was carpeting all over the place but with a big room and linoleum on his floor, why not? Don't become an automatic no-sayer just because someone said no to you. The circumstances may have changed. Second, make sure you're willing to carry the no through at least five minutes of screaming. It's better to say yes in the first place or even, "I wish you wouldn't," than to say no and then to reverse yourself in two minutes. Once a kid finds out he can get a reversal of the verdict by just screaming for two minutes, you've had it.

Onward and upward, or downward, as it is in most houses, to the kitchen.

Take all poisons out of your lower cabinets and put them where the canned foods are. By poison, I mean virtually anything you use to clean anything with—read the back of the package sometime. Then, cleverly, put the canned goods where the cleaning stuff was. It will take a little bending, but think, on the other hand, how nice it will be to find a new sponge without spending twenty minutes searching for it.

Don't leave stepladders around to climb on top of the counter with.

Keep your pots and pans where the kid can get at them. It takes all of thirty seconds to put ten pots back in a cabinet which is a fairly good deal for half an hour's worth of playing.

If you can, try to delegate a corner of the kitchen for play space. Most young children, even those with huge playrooms filled to the brim with toys of every description, would prefer to be near Mommy a lot of the time. Or, if you can spare it, set up a small low drawer for the child. Throw in old or seldom used measuring cups, spoons, coffee measures, a beat-up small percolator; in other words, whatever he gets hold of when you don't want him to. If you don't have a drawer to spare, stick stuff in a box and put it on top of the refrigerator or someplace and bring it out strategically.

It's a good idea to turn pot handles in on the stove. That way, the possibility of the baby pulling a pot of boiling water down on himself is at least minimized. Similarly, there are those of us who feel that, say what you will about all the trouble children are, it's wiser not to leave sharp knives with their handles sticking out over counter tops.

The Royal Chambers

A man's home is his castle and there's no reason why the same shouldn't hold true for a kid. If you want to keep your part of the house relatively free from ruin, TRY to keep the prohibitions to a minimum in his. If it's a rainy day and bubble-blowing is requested, it's nice to have a room where blowing bubbles won't muck up the furniture. This is the place for linoleum, tile, laminated, formica, or enamel painted furniture, dirt-hiding fabrics, and so forth. Keep a painter's dropcloth under the bed or in a closet to spread under an easel or under children who are making miscellaneous messes.

Aside from the emotional problems that may or may not crop up with a new baby and in addition to getting things in shape, there are some specific problems that are somewhat more amenable to solution without the time and trouble of getting shrunk. This doesn't mean that I have some sort of never-fail hint for coping with things like babies who sleep five hours a day—on good days. (Which mine did. I shall never forget sitting over champagne in the hospital room discussing with my husband the benefits of the 7—11—3—7 schedule over the 6—10—2—6. We could have cocktails while I was nursing the baby and then go smilingly arm-in-arm into a yummy dinner that I had whipped up while the baby was taking his four-hour afternoon nap, in between working on the Great American Novel I was writing in all my free time. Actually, the baby's schedule, which seemed to be consistent on alternate Wednesdays, went something like 10—12—2—3:30—5—7—9.*) One of the troubles with caring for a baby is that all of a sudden not only is there a whole other person to take care of, but there are tons of equipment to be curried, cleaned, and what-notted. So I have a few suggestions for saving time (so if you can't write the Great American Novel, at least you can get past page 18 of *The New Yorker* before the next issue comes).

Feeding It: The problem with most babies is not how to get them to eat—most don't develop feeding problems until they're walking—but rather how to get what you consider to be a fair percentage of the stuff actually into their little mouths. You can:

* You are *not* paranoid if you think the baby is doing it on purpose to drive you out of your mind. The chances are fairly good that he's not, but it does make one wonder at times how their radar makes them start crying just when you're sitting down to dinner, or lying down to your husband. The rotten thing is that infants react badly to tension—they pick it up with uncanny aptitude. And the worse they behave the more tense you get and the more tense you get the worse they behave and . . . If you get caught up in this less than ideal situation, if it's remotely possible, a weekend away will generally work wonders. It's hard to believe that anyone would actually *want* to take care of him, or her—but grandparents especially have peculiar tastes.

1. Use bibs, and if you run out of bibs, use towels fastened with a safety pin.

2. Give babies their vitamins in the bath so the dribbles don't stain their clothes.

3. Try teaching them to drink out of a pitcher with a lip before they move on to a cup.

4. Use a cup, rather than a bowl, for soup or cereal.

5. Teach him to feed himself with a spoon by starting with dry cereal instead of something gooey.

6. Put a shower cap on his head while he's eating, although it will probably get yanked off and swooshed around in the food.

Or, if you want to start him out with some nice hangups about eating, you can feed him while he's standing up in the playpen, holding onto the sides for dear life to keep his balance, thus preventing him from grabbing for the spoon.

Clothing It: It should not require too wild a stretching of your belief in psychiatry to accept the formulation that a child is, to a degree, a reflection of its mother. So frequently, a sloppy-looking mother will have a sloppy-looking kid either because Mommy has a poor opinion of herself on the inside and shows it on the outside (and dresses her child accordingly), or Mommy has certain conflicts about her child and not wanting to neglect him in certain rather more important areas like starving him, neglects him in a relatively superficial area like how his clothes look; or Mommy resents the money she has to spend on baby's clothes and dresses him accordingly (there may be ten pretty dresses hanging in the closet, bought when Mommy felt guilty about not dressing her child better, and never worn). It works the other way, too; some mothers who deck out their kids in clothes irrelevant to the situation may be assuming that others are judging them by the way their children are dressed. Of course that's true. We are judged frequently (and sometimes misjudged) on the basis of how our children are dressed, but more often it's more on the basis of how they behave.

It should be unnecessary to point out that you never never never buy anything for a child that needs ironing. Unless you like to iron. However, you are probably stuck with those dumb white shoes. If you care how they look, which I don't except for birthday parties and presentations at court, you can get more mileage if you spray them with hairspray after you've polished them. That way the shoe polish doesn't rub off and they look cleaner longer. If you've let them go for a very long time and polish alone is not enough, you can try getting the dirt off with rubbing alcohol or with a cut raw potato rubbed on the scuffs.

By the way, if the baby is having trouble walking because he slips and slides around on the smooth soles, you can wrap adhesive tape around the bottom which will give him a better grip.

If you're one of the holdouts still using unfolded cloth diapers, you can fold them for the last time when the kid is about twenty pounds and sew them together on your sewing machine. If you're looking for an excuse to switch to Pampers, by the way, I have it on good authority that most diaper companies, in the New York area, at any rate, are controlled by the Mafia. Which leaves you with the dilemma of whether to support the Military-Industrial Complex or Organized Crime.

Paraphernalia: Plastic bottles don't break, as you may have noticed, with anywhere near the regularity of glass ones, so you might switch to them when you're through sterilizing. If you have a dishwasher, it is questionable why exactly you're sterilizing in the first place, since dishwasher water should be hot enough to get the bottles sterile. If you're sterilizing and the doctor said you could stop, maybe you should question why you're doing more than you have to. There is something very satisfying, I think, about sterilizing. It makes one feel very efficient. It is an action that must be done and can be done in a very finite, limited way. Perhaps in boiling up those bottles you're displacing an urge to boil up the baby. Or maybe, if you feel guilty about not breast feeding, it may be a way of showing you're really a terrific mother. At any rate, if you do sterilize you will find after a while that there is an incredible amount of crud in your sterilizer which comes, in case you want to know, from the minerals in the water depositing themselves on the metal. Sterilizing bottles in a cruddy sterilizer has absolutely no effect on how sterile they get. However, it's one of those things that makes you look dirtier than you really are, especially to grand-mothers, and there is a way to clean it, by soaking it overnight to the crud line with water and about a cup and a half of vinegar. Scrub it out in the morning. If it doesn't work, do it again the next night.

If you keep an old empty six-pack that soda came in, you can use it to store bottles and also those bloody baby food jars that proliferate all over your refrigerator.

Against all odds a vast majority of babies survive beyond infancy and grow into what clothing manufac-turers coyly call toddlers, and which books on child care admonishingly call pre-schoolers. The basic line in growing out of babyhood seems to be that the de-mands go from physical ("Pick me up, Mommy) to devious ("Mommy, why can't we go to the zoo today? You promised." "Because it's pouring, that's why." "But Mommy, I could wear my new raincoat and you told me once that you love to walk in the rain" . . .) And so on.

Some people can cope marvelously with babies, but go completely to pieces when it comes to terrible two. Terrible two was best described to me by someone who told me about her little girl who asked for a glass of water. When she got it, she cried. It turned out she wanted ice. So her mother went back to the kitchen and put in a few ice cubes. On receipt, the baby screamed alarmingly. After her mother calmed her down, it turned out that what she wanted was water without ice, only she wanted it with ice.

You can see where some perfectly well-balanced women are driven to drink something other than ice water by the trauma of coping with a two-year-old, who wants what he wants like the devil, but doesn't know what he wants.

What you've got to keep in mind, I think, is that you're probably as good a mother as the rest of the ladies on the park bench and that the same reality testing that's needed to handle housekeeping is vital in raising kids. And the same garbage that affects your ability to keep the house going works toward your mothering as well. If there's resentment toward the child, and there almost always is (maybe there's nothing that makes you say goodbye so definitely to your own childhood as becoming a mother—and that can be hard to take), there may be hostility.

You very likely can't express the hostility directly on the child, so you either displace it to other areas, or make it felt more subtly toward him. Like not dressing him well. Or forgetting to send milk money to school, or leaving knives around on low counters. Even if you're not expressing the hostility in any remarkably offensive way, you still feel guilty about having it, and this frequently takes the form of thinking of yourself as a bad mother and turning the hostility in on yourself. You may go overboard in trying to prove that you're really a terrific mother, doing more than you should and perhaps more than the kid wants. And, as with keeping house, you've got the ghost of your own mother to contend with—the one you knew when you were three or five or nine, who was absolute perfection. She wasn't. Nobody is.

Like it or not, you're probably more concerned with

your own hangups than with anybody else's, and you're sensitized to them. Combine this with the rather natural belief that your child is similar to you, and you may discover your tendency to project your own feelings of inadequacy on him. So, if you were shy as a kid, you're likely to pick up on your child's displays of shyness and exaggerate them.

Since there's consistent feedback between the two of you and since he tends to exaggerate the things he knows you're interested in, you may even be contributing to his picking up the things you don't like about yourself. Just as you may project your fears onto your child, you may project your own aspirations on him as well. Since you see the child as an outgrowth or reflection of yourself, it's not too hard to see how this might happen. But you have got to make some effort to see you and the child as two separate human beings. If you always wanted to be a ballerina, that doesn't mean your daughter has the faintest interest.

The same conspiracy of women that leads you to believe that all women like to do something around the house (and if you don't you're lacking as a woman) is responsible for putting out the rumor that all mothers love their children every minute. Nobody really does. Don't get to feeling all over guilty every time you want to knock his teeth out. Worry about it when you actually do it.

Feeding It: The first thing to bear in mind is that when a child knows you're hung up about his lack of appetite, he will milk it for all it's worth, having latched onto a positively splendid attention-getting device. An attention-getting device means exactly what it sounds like it means, for a change. A kid who knows he can please you and/or get you to look at him and react to him by learning to recite "Twinkle, Twinkle Little Star" backwards in Swahili, will learn how to recite "Twinkle, Twinkle Little Star" backwards in Swahili.

A kid who knows he can get his mother to jump when he cries will cry. And if you really hop to it when he gets a tummyache, he's more likely to get tummyaches than his friend whose mother dismisses tummyaches with a wave of her hand and stands riveted with attention every time he makes a movement. So, if it's at all possible, you've got to play it cool if he's a less than decent eater, pretend total lack of interest in how much he eats and keep conversation on food down to a minimum.

This is all very nice and sensible but when all evidence points to the conclusion that your child is eating considerably less than his pet hamster, you may find it difficult to maintain a calm, unruffled exterior as he makes do for dinner on a one-inch-square piece of cheese. Manfully, for three and one half years I stuck to it. I swore before I had children that I'd never force them to eat, going on the not unreasonable assumption that no middle-class American Jewish child has ever died of starvation. And if they're really hungry they'll eat.

But a two-year hunger strike, along with our son's being the runt of his nursery school class, finally wore me down, raised my guilt to an intolerable level, and I became a common food pusher, using all the low, mean, rotten tricks of the trade. It helps to tell yourself over and over that there is as much nourishment in a hamburger as in two bites of steak. It also helps to serve positively minuscule portions. It also helps to use bribes and threats, but that is adding insult to injury or injury to insult so although I have to admit to doing it I shouldn't recommend it. On the other hand, it does work better than anything else and everybody else does it and it's all in the kid's interest, right?

If the problem is less getting them to eat it and more getting them to eat it without their turning your stomach while they do it, you may have some success with merely recontainering things like:

sugar in a salt shaker,
milk in a syrup pitcher,
juice in a closed pitcher with a small pouring hole,
ketchup and mustard in those ghastly squeeze-type
bottles.

I break my kids in on restaurant manners by blowing them to lunch once a month or so at the local
variety store. It's a relatively cheap etiquette course.

That takes care of getting it in and keeping most of
it off the floor. For cleanup, where little kids seem to
have the fantasy that you have just dipped the washcloth in lye, it might help to tell them that you're only
going to clean off the potatoes or the kumquat-guava
juice, or whatever you happened to serve as part of
dinner. This is emphatically not recommended for kids
who do it themselves, who are smartasses and who will
do exactly that.

If you don't feel like cutting out a chunk of a new
hairdo, chewing gum can be removed from heads by
working in a glob of cold cream and then squooshing
the whole mess out. You can also do it with peanut
butter, I understand, but that sounds unbelievably disgusting. Personally, I whack it out with a scissors and
nobody has ever yet commented on their less than
perfect coiffures.

Getting Him to Sleep: I think that most babies and
little kids respond to parental demands and desires
on which Mommy and/or Daddy place a relatively
high degree of importance. Think back to the stuff
about superegos where we pointed out that kids react
to verbal stimuli, but what they picked up subliminally,
as it were, counts, too. We feel, my husband and I,
that getting up before 8:00 in the morning is a hard-
ship only slightly less awful than having to spend an
evening with my great aunt and uncle (the rich ones)
whose idea of a good time is to show movies they took
of the urban renewal project up the block after a dinner

of boiled vegetables and a festive drink of Cherry Heering. In fact, we achieved a small amount of celebrity in our set for our ability to sleep late B.C. (Before Child). Friends used to call us at three on a Sunday afternoon, expressing the hope that they hadn't awakened us. So when this year-old baby began waking up at six in the morning, I merely walked in several times and said in a definitely firm and unfriendly voice, "We do not get up at this hour in this house." That may have been what did it. On the other hand, it may have been the cookies I tossed in around 11:00 P.M. along with a fresh bottle of apple juice. You can do that sort of thing if you're relatively desperate with a baby.

Slightly later comes the I-wanna-drinka-water ploy. We have solved this by putting a glass of water on the bedside table. I heard of someone who ties a canteen on the bedpost. Now it is perfectly true that it isn't really water that the kid is after, but rather attention. It's just a matter of where you draw your particular line on hours when attention is given.

One other thing I've heard of which sounds intriguing for a kid of four to six or so is to establish a rule along the lines of "You go to sleep at the same hour you get up," i.e., if he starts jumping on your stomach at six in the morning, he is put summarily to bed at six in the evening. I think this takes a special sort of child, of which mine is distinctly not one.

Dressing Him: The same baby boy who uncomplainingly wore lace dresses and curls may turn into a kid who thinks that wearing anything other than his jeans, with which he has developed a mystical relationship, is akin to having to eat something that is not hamburger. Somewhere there lies a middle ground where resides happiness. Lots of luck finding it.

Don't get hooked into the buy-them-a-size-larger syndrome, which produces kids who spend half their time looking like baggy-drawered circus clowns and the other half like junior versions of skid row in worn-out tatters. However, it is remarkable that when you finally decide to buy clothes that fit, they finally decide to have a growth spurt.

Marking things, one of life's drabber occupations, can be considerably shortened, if not exactly brightened, by marking clothes with a rubber stamp and an indelible ink pad. Also, if you dip a Q-tip in Clorox, you can write names on boots and rubbers—provided they're not white. It romoves the color from the rubber.

You don't have to drag the kid to the store every time if you bring along another of the article you want—say a shirt that fits him well. You just match it up.

If it bothers you, you can get rid of the white line when you let down jeans, if you let down jeans, by running a dark blue crayon over the line.

If you're instructing in the fine art of learning to button buttons, teach them to start with the bottom button. It's easier.

Cleaning Him: I always take a strong drink into the bathroom when giving a shampoo. I also have another when I've finished. I have it on the authority of the head barber at the most elegant children's barber shop in New York that you don't have to shampoo children's hair at all, provided you get a wet hot washcloth, wring it out well, and rub it over the kid's hair every night. This assumes that you prefer going through minor hell every night, as opposed to major hell once a week.

If you do go through major hell once a week, or once a month, several things might help:

shampoo goggles, if you can find them,

cold cream smeared on the eyebrows, which deflects the water away from the delicate little eyes,

a rubber hose attachment for the faucet, which doubles as a handy thing to beat the child with if he won't let you shampoo him.

Compared to shampoos, baths are child's play, which brings up the problem of what to do with all those toys, particularly if you share the same bath and your husband does not dig bathing with a rubber duck. A string bag on a hook is a good toy collector.

If your child shows no overwhelming desire to degrease himself by himself, a soap mitt, which you can make if you can't find one in the drugstore, may make the whole idea almost appealing.

Taking Them Somewhere: Train them as early as possible to sit in the back. This is (a) safer, and (b) allows you and your husband to communicate to a limited degree. If it's a longish trip and naps are indicated and devoutly to be wished for, you can save taking a pillow if you take a pillow case and stuff it with clothes to be laundered. (You use your discretion and do not stuff it with dirty diapers.) If your travel companion is of jump-rope age, a jump-rope stop now and then helps get rid of that excess energy that so frequently is misdirected into seeing which finger fits best in baby's eyeball. If you take crayons and if you happen to have around where you can find it an old oblong cakepan with a lid, the crayons fit nicely inside and the top is a good surface to draw on.

If you're just going across town to a movie or something with more than one kid and it's wintertime, it would not be a bad idea to take along a shopping bag in which to put coats, hats, scarves, and toys brought from home that the child believes are necessary to keep him from being attacked by vampires.

Very Miscellaneous Time and Trauma Savers

If you are bothered by a little child coming to you with a record in hand and saying "What is this?" you could paste on the label part a picture of three little pigs (provided the record happened to be "The Three Little Pigs"). This is a relatively big project, so you'd better be really bothered.

If you have a child learning to roller skate, adhesive tape on the wheels will slow down the action and he will fall less and you will have to pick him up less and put Band Aids on less, so it pays.

If your second Christmas is rolling around, you can stick the tree in the playpen where it will at least not be pulled down. Probably. Around the third or fourth Christmas, you could give the kid its own tree, some tinsel and some unbreakable cheap ornaments, and he might just keep his grubby hands off your hand-painted two-hundred-year-old baubles.

You can fix a small alarm clock onto the handles of his bike if he's something less than ideal about getting home when you told him to. This assumes, however, that he will (a) heed the warning, and (b) be anywhere near his bike when the bell tolls.

If he is deplorable about having his picture taken, you can get him to work on putting the dog or cat or compost heap into suitable shape for having its picture taken. Then, while he's all involved in getting the stupid dog to shake hands, you snap away.

Ask Not What You Can Do for Your Child . . .

To say that anything goes in a child's room is not quite the same as saying that it should look constantly as though Romper Room School had just let out. Children from the age of two should be encouraged to keep their rooms tidy, i.e., pick up the junk before they get out some more. Children around this age are developing a natural and—sometimes when it involves screaming if you've moved a piece of furniture in the back bedroom from its customary place—an infuriating tendency toward order. If you can find a way to harness it, you should be out working on peaceful uses for atomic power. Some of you may be aware that there is a certain amount of reluctance on the part of some children to pick up. One way to make it easier is to have a general organization for the room. If trucks go in this bin, and dolls in this, it's a lot easier than if this red truck here goes next to that yellow car and two inches behind the blue bus. After all, what you're after is the ability to walk through the room without serious danger to life or limb, and enough organization to permit the kid to find his own toys. Generally, the larger the receptacle, the easier it is for a child to put things away—just think how easy it would be if you just told him to toss it all in the closet.

Vegetable bins that stack make much better holders for toys of many parts than the boxes they come in. Plastic refrigerator containers are much easier for a pre-schooler to put crayons into than a crayon box (you try it). A record rack makes a better book shelf than a book shelf.

Who knows why it is that children have so many toys—do parents give their children material objects to make up for a lack of affection? Do grandparents shower grandchildren with toys because they want to give them what they couldn't give their own children? Is it a rebuke from grandparents to their own children or a way of winning their grandchildren's undying love? But there are several ways of coping with the toy explosion:

1. Never buy, and encourage relatives never to buy, any toy consisting of more than three parts if there are any children under five years old in the house.

2. Two or three times a year, weed out. Get two big cartons, put in the toys that never seem to get played with, and stick them on top of a closet. In the other carton stick all the toys with missing parts and

toss the parts in as you find them. If you really truly think you might ever do it, you can make a third carton of toys that need to be fixed and deliver it to your husband to be worked on during half-times during the winter. Or grit your teeth and throw them out. Bring back the good toys after three or four months. Some children can be conned into believing they're getting a whole lot of new toys. Some.

3. Try the "Anything I have to pick up goes into the top of my closet and you won't get it back for a week" routine. This has worked for some people but must be said in a firm but friendly voice. Also you have to stick to it (it doesn't have to be a week, a day will do).

4. Work along with the kid. For some reason, sharing a pick-up of loony links means more to a kid than if you pick up the Loony Links and he picks up the Silly Sponge.

5. Say, "If you can't take care of your toys then I will take them all away and give them to the poor children who would be happy to have them and would take good care of them. When I was a child I didn't have half the toys you have." Oh, go on and say it. How do you know it won't work?

In the course of researching this book, I've come across several hints on how to get little kids to clean up after themselves. All of which I have tried on my five-year-old and none of which have worked. However, children being what they are, perhaps one of the following will appeal to your child's particular sense of responsibility:

You can hide pennies around which are his to find in the course of dusting or picking up. Mine just picked up the pennies, fastidiously extracting them from a floor full of his toys.

You can play music and have him pick something up each time the music stops. This is more trouble than it's worth. So is making a laundry bag out of net and attaching it to a rounded wire coat hanger and having him throw his dirty clothes in there instead of into a hamper.

If you have more than one kid, you can write the titles of jobs on little slips of paper, and shake them all up in a coffee can, if you can find one, and let them pick out things that say "vacuum the dog" or "clean your room." It's probably a good idea to make one out of five slips something like "get a piece of gum" or "victimize your baby sister."

While we're on the subject of getting him off his bottom to clean up his own mess, there's something to be said for the proposition that everyone should pull his own weight in the house, even if it's only twenty-five pounds. Remember that young children really want to be like you—before they're a year old, babies are propping themselves up on toy carpet sweepers, lurching after Mommy as she listlessly pushes her hateful grown-up toy in front of her. The only trouble is that, not being particularly adept at carrying out commands more complex than four words or three seconds long, this marvelous imitative drive usually winds up causing more trouble than it's worth.

Don't expect much from your child until he's around three, but by then he should be keeping his room reasonably neat, when nagged relentlessly. By five he should require a mere raising of the voice and a simple threat like, "If you don't get your room picked up before dinner you won't get any dessert." It is unfortunate that around this age a child learns that he can get a lot of mileage out of saying, "That's okay, I don't want any dessert. You make crappy desserts anyway." Note how he is already displacing his hostility onto your cooking ability. Think of how threatened you feel. This brings us into the whole rotten subject of discipline. Which I don't feel like talking about right now but might later. After five years of close laboratory study of children I have concluded that there are only two workable forms of discipline and in doing so have thrown out all books on child psychology: (1) bribes, and (2) threats. You must be very, very clever and know exactly what your child cares about, however. Although a threat like, "If you don't stop watching television right now this very minute I won't let you go to dancing class tomorrow" has a certain value in throwing him off the scent of your particular way of frontally attacking.

Ask not what you can do for your children. Ask what your children can do for you. Somewhere around four, he can set the table. The demitasse spoons may occupy the fish fork place, and the claret glass may stand to the wrong side of the water goblet, but he can do a creditable job. At first you'll have to hand him three plates and say, "Now darling, put one plate by Mommy . . ." By the time he's five he should be able to get the stuff out by himself. You have now delegated table setting to someone else and have therefore less work to do than before you had children.

The same child of five or so can do a lot of things to help you:

He can load clothes from a hamper into the washing machine.

He can get things for you (like your wallet from the bedroom, the baby's bottle from the kitchen).

He can stir together ingredients in a bowl.

He can do a crummy job of sweeping and a mediocre job of dusting.

He can start to learn to make his bed in the morning.

He can sort silverware.

He can wipe up things you've spilled.

He can wash vegetables and shell peas.

He can wash out his paintbrushes.

In other words, he can do a remarkable number of things. Whether or not he will do them depends on how much time you're willing to devote to teaching him how.

You've spent years learning how to do all the extra new tasks that come with having kids and learning how to do them efficiently. Although it's certainly quite true that a child won't do something if it's being done for him, you have to decide how much it's worth to you. When you add up the hours it takes to help a child learn to button a button, you may conclude that it's much easier to button the bloody button yourself. Maybe it is, maybe it's not. It depends on whether you go in for long-term gains vs. short-term losses or the other way around. If it's occurred to you to wait until he gets to kindergarten to learn to tie his shoes, where his teachers will teach him, sparing you the time and trouble, you aren't the only one. It's quite probable that by the time he gets to Harvard he will know how to tie his own shoelaces or at least he will have acquired the intelligence to wear loafers.

Sick Kids and also hurt ones, which can sometimes be worse

If you have to give bad-tasting medicine, you can plan for the long range by giving vitamins with a spoon instead of a dropper from the very beginning. That way, when it's time to dose them with something truly disgusting, you just slip it to them in a spoon, which they do not immediately associate with icky stuff. If you are unfortunately without a new baby right now to break in, you can try having them suck on an ice cube, which numbs the taste buds. Also, if your child gets a cut lip, as what child does not, a Popsicle inserted in the mouth works two ways to stop tears. Should you be motivated, by the way, to stop tears in a little kid, take a bottle and enlist the kid's co-operation in collecting some tears to save. This is one of those rather corny things that seem to work quite nicely. Another sneaky measure for common catastrophes is to keep a red or black washcloth (but preferably red, since you probably don't have a black one around either and have to go out and buy one) by the sink where you wash off bloody wounds. Somehow, not seeing all the gore on a light-colored washcloth reduces the degree of trauma considerably. (It's worth pointing out that just as being picky about food can sometimes be a child's idea of how to get some attention, the same holds true for scraped knees that get an attentive audience from Mommy or Daddy. It may explain why there are so many accident-prone people around.)

My husband the doctor recommends that you go out to a surgical supply house and buy a tweezers, otherwise known as a bayonet clamp, which makes removing splinters fantastically easier. If you run across a splinter that's hard to locate, especially after the kid has pointed to six different places as the seat of his agony, wash the area (where it is, nine times out of ten, very filthy) carefully and paint around where you suspect the splinter to be embedded with Merthiolate or iodine. The splinter should then show up as a dark sliver.

The big question is, how do you keep them in bed after they've seen "Sesame Street" and it's only 10:00 A.M.? The real question to answer first is do they have to stay in bed? Before you let yourself in for one of the worst sieges of motherhood—keeping a kid in bed —make sure it's necessary. Check with your doctor. As it happens, I've been able to let my kids remain ambulatory in clothes, albeit not run any hundred-yard dashes, with fevers up to a hundred and five.

If you *like* keeping him in bed, give a thought to the possibility that you're using his illness as a way to be supermother in an area where you're gifted. Especially if he seems to get sicker than most kids and really wants to stay in bed. He may have latched onto the knowledge that getting sick is another great attention-getting device.

However, assuming that there's a reason or a medical

order to confine them between the sheets, there are a few small things you can do to make life more bearable for the kid and coincidentally more bearable for you, too. It's interesting to contemplate whether the super-niceness mothers deal out to sick kids is not a kind of reaction formation to the real resentment they feel at having to take care of them. In any case, there are more interesting routes to martyrdom.

Stock a bedside table with necessary paraphernalia—tissues, a pitcher and glass, and something to drink if the child is old enough to pour without spilling; a thermometer and vaseline, and whatever else your little invalid needs. The main idea is to keep from having to run relay races forty-seven times a day with the latest in royal fiats. If the paraphernalia is really involved, you might stick a lazy susan on the table if you have one, so that the child can rotate it and not ask you for something that's three inches out of his feeble reach.

A wastebasket by the side of the bed is ineffably more esthetic than picking sneezed-into tissues off it, one by one, six times a day.

A table for eating or playing is handy. If you don't happen to have a white wicker breakfast tray from Fortnum and Mason that came with your English breakfast china, or an old hospital bed left over from your sick grandmother's last visit, you can use your ironing board, pushed down to a convenient height, with the narrow end over the bed.

Speaking of eating, if the kid's appetite has gone from birdlike to mosquito-like, you might try serving meals in a muffin tin, of all things. This makes things less spilly (you can put what's to drink in one of the sections) and it gives you a wonderful opportunity to rack your brain for appealingly edible things to stick in the compartments—like smoked pigeon tongues, or strawberries in February, that he might deign to eat and keep his strength up with.

If you have the fortitude, you can save out a bunch

of desirable toys and produce them with a flourish when there's a sick kid. This does not mean a box of rejects and dolls with two arms missing, since most kids are even more demanding when they're sick than when they're well.

This may have something to do with the mechanism of regression that crops up in most sick people—adult or kid. You can view it as a threat that is met with a return to an easier and less demanding life (like your husband who demands to be waited on like a child when he comes down with a case of the flu just like the one you went through last week without even mentioning).

In adults a tendency to take to one's bed when the going gets rough is not precisely unheard of, but is a luxury that few women with children can afford. Which may be why so few mothers ever get sick—there's absolutely no percentage in it. Can you see yourself walking into your baby's room one morning and saying, "I'm awfully sorry, Herbert. I just don't feel very well this morning and I think I'll take the day off from work." In any case, you've got to remember that little kids are frequently confused by being sick and scared beyond all proportion to the condition—especially if it happens when they're going through a stage of being all hung up about their bodies. They can even think they're going to die. Or that something they did that was naughty just caught up with them and made them sick. (You can see how some fantasies get started.) So it's a kindly gesture to at least listen to their nutty questions and give an answer if you can.

An old shirt of yours or your husband's makes a great home hospital gown if there's a lot of throwing up or spilling staining medicine or if you just didn't get around to washing out the pajamas.

If you desperately need a humidifier and yours is broken because you forgot to clean it for the last two years, you can use your electric coffee maker with the inside parts and top removed. Fill it with water and plug it in by the bed. This assumes that your electric coffee maker is working.

When it comes to teeth, I am somewhat fatalistic about the whole thing. I'm convinced that you're either born with good ones or you're born with bad ones, and it's all predetermined about when the sperm hits the egg. My mother, for instance, kept a toothbrush at the ready and got me virtually every time I opened my mouth, and the best I could ever do after a visit to the dentist was come home and say, "Look, Ma, only twelve cavities." I rebelled in college by brushing my teeth once a week for the first month until my roommate gently told me that there were other reasons besides fewer cavities for brushing after meals. My husband, on the other hand, came home after his first visit to the dentist in eight years with a clean bill of health, which caused me to gnash my teeth enough to probably produce a misalignment somewhere. On the other hand, he had to wear braces, which I didn't. My children, unfortunately, take after me. Michael is the only child I know who was a veteran of root canal work by the age of four.

However, having been brainwashed into believing that frequent toothbrushing and a careful program of dental hygiene, and a less than constant candy consumption, keeps the old decay down, I pass on two toothbrushing hints, good for five- or six-year-olds who are naive enough to believe in the tooth fairy and who find the sight of a toothbrush about as appealing as the sight of a rectal thermometer. (Do you think there's some Freudian significance to that? Some equivalent fear of penetration in both cases?) You might put across the story that the tooth fairy, being a shrewd manipulator, shells out very little money for damaged merchandise and pays a whole dollar for ones without cavities or fillings.

I have had some limited success with what we call

the Sunday Box in our house. The idea is that all candy accumulated in the course of a week (do you think it's the town dentist who supplies all the town merchants with lollipops?) goes into this box and on Sunday after lunch a veritable orgy of candy gorging is permitted. There is, believe it or not, a limit to the amount of candy a child can consume in one sitting.

VI

How Would You Like Two Weeks in Paris With All Expenses Paid

OR,
DO YOU REALLY WANT A MAID?

You do not want a maid if you're quite content with the state of your house. And you do not want a maid if you don't feel at all put upon by the job of house-keeping. Otherwise, if you're breathing, you probably do. Assuming that you do want a maid, and assuming you're in the market for one and you've been toying with the idea of going out every other Tuesday to sell your body to make the money to afford one, there are a few things you should bear in mind before taking the plunge.

1. There are some disadvantages to having a maid.
2. A good maid is hard to find.
3. Once you have found her, never letting her go may take a lot of doing.

Taking them one by one:

First, the disadvantages. *There's a lack of privacy.* It's not so much that you can't walk around in the

108

buff, as it's hard to sit and read a magazine when someone is slogging away at your dirty oven. Telephone conversations have to be kept at a low level sometimes, love letters hidden, and so on. A not inconsiderable number of maids do love to talk about one employer to another, so if you share a maid with a friend or acquaintance, expect some feedback.*

Personal Involvement

Involvement is something you may not run up against if you're out of the house when your maid is in. If you communicate by note then you're not too likely to be informed that her brother-in-law has just hijacked a plane to Cuba. But if you're around when she's around, a certain amount of human contact is going to go on between the two of you after awhile. You may, like Daphne back in Chapter I, be the sort of person who finds it difficult to maintain a sympathetic attitude while listening to the problems of someone you don't care too much about. Or, like Betty, who complains of not wanting some stranger to mess around with her things and who may be expressing her distaste for personal involvement on any level. If you've been avoiding getting a maid for this reason, you might consider a cleaning service. A man, or a team of men, comes to your house every week or however often you like and does your bidding. More highly trained than daily cleaning women, they generally maintain a highly professional attitude and would panic if you wanted to ask them about their personal lives. Check the yellow pages of your telephone book to locate one.

---

* Of course it works the other way around. You can pick up some juicy bits about your friends and enemies once you've won your maid's confidence.

Dependency

If your maid is any good at all, you're going to be in a hell of a lot of trouble if she leaves you. On the other hand, worrying about whether and when a maid that you haven't hired yet is going to quit strikes me as somewhat pessimistic. For many women, a maid takes on some of the characteristics of mother. I have one friend who severed virtually all ties with her mother and yet continues to share the same maid, one who was with her family since childhood and to whom she is positively devoted. Having a maid (mother) around your house may set off some conflicts about your role and your competition with your mother. This is exacerbated if you happen to be a dependent type like Topsy. If, like Betty, who is possibly directing a whole lot of her time and energy to proving she's a better woman than her mother ever was because deep down she doubts it so much, the conflicts of competing may make you uptight.

Loss of Excuse

Maids take away the last, best excuse for being tired, having a messy house, being a failure at your job. And of course you have to excuse yourself to you as well as to your family. It's easy to dismiss your fatigue or failure on the basis of not having help. When you get it and you're still failing, you're forced to question your failure more comprehensively.

Overcompensating

Ostensibly, you hire a maid to lighten your work load. Watch out for a tendency to work just as much if not more on things that you didn't have time for before. If you hire someone and you're still putting in as many hours, you'd better reevaluate. Either she's a lousy maid or you haven't come to terms with the problem of how much you require yourself to do. You have to divorce the real needs of your house from your own needs to express your emotions through it. Some women, who feel guilty about having to get help with their house, wear themselves out over trivia to make up for the big jobs they're not doing any more. Others clean the house the night before she comes, as if to deny their need for her (which might also relate to their denial of their need for a mother, as well).

Assuming that you feel that you can handle the emotional ramifications of having somebody work for you, you're ready for the second hurdle.

HOW TO FIND A MAID

Most women get their maids from a friend, or from a friend of a friend. Or maybe the doorman in an apartment house knows that one of the tenants has a maid who wants to work another day. Uusually, there's a casual or desperate conversation with someone you know whose maid has just mysteriously freed up a day. The advantages are quite obvious. She comes recommended. The disadvantages are not quite so obvious. And maids have probably broken up more friendships than dry cleaners have broken up marriages.

Let's suppose that your friend Sue recommends Martha, her once-a-week maid, and you and Martha, having chatted enough over the phone to discern that it is possible at least that you will be able to tolerate each other, agree that she will lighten your load every Thursday from "around nine" till whenever she gets through. "Whenever she gets through." Inevitably old Martha is going to fail to show up one fine day (and somehow it will be the morning after the night before when for the first time in your life, so help you God, you said the hell with it and went to bed with a sink full of dishes, drinks on the table, and an ashtray knocked over on the middle of the living room rug. If you're really cursed, she may stand you up on the day of your yearly cocktail party). Now this is bad enough, but when she calls you up two days later (63 percent of maids cannot be reached on the telephone) to confess that her absence was caused by a broken collarbone suffered when she was attacked by a pack of mad dogs that roam Central Park, it should be clear, even to a less than giant intellect, that she is not going to show up at Sue's on Monday. If you and old Martha are not making it, it's somehow beyond her ability to cook up a reason why she has to quit you and still be able to work for Sue. Presto. No maid for you and none for Sue, who hates you when she realizes you've unwittingly done her out of a cleaning lady. Maids feel guilty, too, you know.

Maids can, of course, be gotten from other sources, most notably an agency. If you have a state employment agency in your area, check with them, since they're often a good source. If you get a maid from an agency, you should ask to see and be shown references. The form with references is to accentuate the positive and eliminate the negative so read them with a view to what has not been mentioned—honesty and reliability are omissions that should make you quite leery of employing somebody.

Live-in help is getting harder to find and when and if you find it, be prepared to pay. It makes financial sense for some people who have household help three days and hire a lot of expensive baby sitters in addition. But every disadvantage of having a maid goes triple if you've got her living in your home.

Fringe Benefits

If you try to think of yourself as a boss and your maid as your employee, you may avoid some of the hangups that go with having a servant. Contrary to what some people appear to believe, maids are people. More specifically, they are people doing a job. Like any other group of workers, some are good and some are bad, some are fat and some are thin, some are fast and some are slow, some want to get ahead, some want to stay where they are. The things that differentiate maids from many other groups of workers are:

1. They are servants working directly for one person. There are hangups that go along with giving orders, if you're not used to doing it, and taking orders, if you don't like to do so. One thing that affects the relationship is that the money comes directly from you; it's different in business. If your husband has an incompetent secretary at least he doesn't think about the things he could be buying with the money he'd save if he fired her.

2. Few women are able to relate to a maid in the most tenable way—that is as employer to employee—and for that reason they're uncomfortable in the master-slave relationship in which they see themselves. The best way to structure things is to think of yourself as a boss and your maid as your employee, and to offer fringe benefits that are humane. As with pay scale, you ought to check with your friend, but perhaps the two of you can work something out. Most of the people I know pay their maids for about one tenth of days sick, i.e., if she works one day a week she gets five sick days a year; three times a week, perhaps fifteen sick days. It is, after all, about what one expects in an office. Christmas bonuses, periodic raises, and summer vacations are unfortunately considered by most women great

largesse. They aren't and shouldn't be, but let your conscience and your community guide you. Perhaps when the job is minimally dignified with minimal benefits, more women will consider it a reasonable form of employment.

Before we get into the arcane erudition necessary to learning how to train your maid to be the envy of all your friends, there's a fairly important subject to consider. It's a pretty solid reality that many domestic workers today are black. It's also true that many housewives and career women deplore the fact that black women are virtually forced into this role. This leads to an interesting development, a curious manifestation of liberal guilt and doublethink. There are basically three ways of coping with this problem:

1. Comb your town for a white domestic worker whom you can ask to do menial tasks because it is, after all, what you're paying her for.

2. Convince yourself that it is inverse prejudice to treat a black employee any differently from the way you'd treat a white one if you'd gotten one.

3. Try to structure the job so that it's as much as possible like an employer/employee relationship. Go back and read the note about fringe benefits again.

The most common problem many women find themselves with when employing a black maid is that, because of feelings of guilt, justified or not, the relationship becomes one of asking favors. Once the relationship has deteriorated to one of, "Martha, I'm having some people over tonight, would you mind awfully getting the living room rug vacuumed?", you're a dead duck. If you had a black secretary you bloody well wouldn't be asking her if she'd mind awfully much if it were possible sometime this afternoon when she got a minute to put through a long distance call for you. Or if you did you wouldn't have a job for very long. And she'd probably get yours and you'd at least have advanced the cause of civil rights. That's why it's essential to let your domestic employee know as precisely as possible what her job involves.

Another thing to avoid is largesse. Dat ol' debil guilt again. Unless you can carry it off, and most women can't, it's better not to offer handouts—unless they're very very good. If you had tickets to a show that you couldn't use you might offer them to your secretary, but you sure as hell wouldn't offer her your old belt with the broken buckle. Gifts are easy to take, charity isn't. If your children outgrow their clothing, it's far better to tell your maid that "Look, there's a bunch of stuff at the back of Mary's closet that she's outgrown. Why don't you take a look through it and if you know any- one who can use it please take it," than to hand her the precious garments one by one. If you're getting rid of some furniture and it's not too motheaten, you can offer it. Just steer clear of junk.

Don't lend money—unless it's a relatively small sum that can be paid back easily within a couple of months. Fifty dollars can be paid back by deducting ten dollars a week for five weeks. A hundred dollars with no set pay-back plan can lead to problems. You may lose your money, but, even worse, you may lose a good maid.

Don't flaunt it. Don't leave bankbooks showing $50,000 balances casually lying around. Don't complain about the impossibility of finding a decent chair for under five hundred dollars. Don't discuss money any more than you can help it. "Thank God the tuition at Herbert's nursery school only went up a hundred dol- lars" is a perfectly inoffensive statement when made to a friend. Think of how it sounds to someone whose kid goes to an inner-city school and to whom a hundred bucks is a small fortune.

Don't talk politics unless you really mean it, or she really means it, or you really believe in what you're saying and aren't doing it just to show her what a good guy you are. A statement that begins, "Of course, what the blacks really need," is an affront.

In short, just because you're employing a black woman, don't go all over guilty that you're the master and she's the slave.

Before you hire a maid you should have some idea of what she's coming for. If you want someone to thoroughly clean an eight-room house in one day a week, you'd better look for Superwoman. You might be able to get some idea from the following chart of about how many maid hours are required to keep a house in smooth and clean order. This is, of course, exclusive of washing, ironing, taking care of kids, and mulching the roses. It also presupposes that you've gotten hold of someone who, if not the demon dirt destroyer, is at least competent.

3 rooms	½ day
4 rooms	1 day
5 rooms (2 baths)	1½ days
7 rooms (3 baths)	2 days

Add one day for each additional three rooms. Add ½ day for each two young children (they make more fingerprints, open the refrigerator more often, and, well, if you have them, you know).

This assumes that you want a maid for cleaning. Now you may have no objection to, say, keeping up the bedroom yourself, in which case you could either save some money and have your maid fewer hours or get her to do the laundry or polish the silver in her left-over time.

If you have children you may have given some thought to hiring a maid to do some babysitting on the side. This seems like a very tempting idea—you get double your money's worth. She cleans while she watches the baby. It's a combination that doesn't work out a lot of the time, however. In the first place, she isn't as used to your baby as you are and she may find it genuinely more difficult to clean and watch the baby than you do. Second, there are few maids who wouldn't prefer babysitting to scrubbing floors, so you may notice that the balance shifts and you've got yourself a baby-sitter who cleans a little, rather than a maid who looks after the baby a little. So make it clear from the start whether or not you expect child care to be one of her duties, and if you opt for this prepare for the possibility of perhaps one-half efficiency. If you simply want to leave the baby with her occasionally, perhaps for a couple of hours during the nap, it's considerate to ask her if she'd mind, rather than grandly assuming that she considers it part of her job. She may hate children, for all you know.

When the Doorbell Rings

First thing to do is to find out her last name—and use it. Of course, if she really doesn't like it—it may never have happened to her before—you can't. Be polite, take her coat, thank her for coming. Don't gush, don't tell her that you've been waiting for her in a state of agitated excitement. Don't attempt to explain to her why you've hired her; there is something offensive about a sentence like, "Since the baby came I don't seem to have my old get-up-and-go, and even with the baby nurse, it's difficult to keep up the apartment." For all you know she has three children under two at home, one a paraplegic and one a three-month-old baby who kept her up all last night with colic. In fact, I'd say that it's a pretty fair bet that your maid has a lot more problems than you have, so if you want to avoid resentment, steer clear of your own.

The thesis is that people will work harder for people they like. You're probably reasonably likeable, so if you don't come on like an ogre, the chances are she'll want to please you—beyond the simple desire to get or keep a job. Courtesy dictates, and a small amount of projecting yourself into her place would seem to necessitate, some kind of getting-to-know-you action. Offering her a cup of coffee and sitting down and expressing an interest in her life probably won't kill you and if yours is going to be, you hope, a long and fruitful relationship, you might as well start it on a basis of genuine if limited friendship. You might find a topic of mutual interest other than your house, to kick off the discussion—like, how was the trip to your house, or how many children does she have, or what your children are like or whether she thinks it will stop snowing before evening. Avoid talking about things like how awful it was that that nice Martin Luther King got shot, he was a credit to his race.

It's vital to discuss with her her salary and fringe benefits, the hours or days she's working, what if any are her duties beyond cleaning (laundry, babysitting, how you like your phone calls answered, and so on) as well as whether or not she expects you to pay withholding taxes. If your husband is around, or your kids, introduce her and just because she's your servant doesn't mean she's your kids' servant, too. She's an older woman and she'll get respect of a sort from the kids if you introduce her as someone who's going to be doing a job in the house.

Once you've gotten the basic amenities out of the way it's time to get down to the nitty gritty. She is, after all, there to clean. Don't give her an all-encompassing guided tour the first day, pointing out where the ashtrays go and what piece of sheet music will go on the piano.

Presumably, you've made a list before of what you want her to do and where you want her to begin. You should know the places of most importance to you, although, in the interest of good employer/employee relations, it is perhaps advisable not to begin with an order to clear out the dead cockroaches from the kitchen cabinets. Try to give her some realistic idea of what you hope she'll accomplish. She can pace herself better if she knows what you expect her to do.

Hopefully you've made up your mind about what you want her to do—either she's going to do as much of everything as she can, or she's going to be assigned to the specific jobs you loathe the most. Begin by showing her where you keep your cleaning equipment, which hopefully you've put in some semblance of order—you wouldn't like it too much if you walked into a job to find a typewriter without a ribbon and a carton filled with eighteen different kinds of stationery, none of which had a demonstrable purpose. Remember, she's a professional and these are her tools. This is not to say you have to be outfitted like a combination hardware store and supermarket. Point out the idiosyncrasies, if any, of your equipment and ask her if there's anything you don't have that she particularly likes to use. If your cleaning equipment is decently organized (consider labeling attachments of your vacuum cleaner and, if you're really motivated, never at home, or cursed with a procession of different maids every other week, put directions on boxes, bottles, and so forth) you'll get far more efficient work from your maid.

If she's going to start a specific job like defrosting the refrigerator, you can merely tell her it's first on the agenda and assume she knows how to do it. If it's more nebulous, like cleaning the living room, it's a bit more complex. You have your own way of doing things and she has hers and who's to say whose is better. It's better not to say something like, "Could you vacuum the rug, then wash the floor, then . . . etc." Rather a statement like, "This room needs a thorough cleaning. Could you pay special attention to the woodwork? I usually do the walls first."

Assume the best. Assume she knows how to clean a house, probably better than you do. Let her know what's important to you, tell her if the old antique rocking bathtub requires the attention of old antique rocking bathtub polish and let her rip. It's a good idea to suggest that she put anything whose whereabouts are in doubt in a pile on top of something. There is absolutely nothing wrong with checking up on your maid to see how she's doing. Especially if two hours have passed since she entered the bathroom. You're allowed to criticize, too—but keep two things in mind:

A compliment takes the bite out of a criticism, and

You're not going to change her style. Not in one day anyway.

Let's suppose you've turned her loose in the bedroom with instructions to vacuum the furniture, wipe off the woodwork, and polish the furniture. After a reasonable time, say half an hour, sidle in and look for something nice to say. Maybe, "Gosh, you really got a lot of dirt off the woodwork," or "My antimacassars haven't looked this good in years." Then if there's something she's doing wrong, or didn't do, bring it up. "I think you missed the legs on that table." Don't be apologetic if she's used the wrong polish on the table, just point it out to her. If she's doing something in a way you don't, you can ask her why she's doing it that way—you might learn something.

After one room, or at the most half a day's work, if you look for the signs, you'll probably find that your maid falls into one of the following categories:

1. Fast and sloppy
2. Slow and thorough
3. Fast and thorough
4. Slow and sloppy
5. Stupid

If you've hooked a number 3 type, hold onto her for dear life, for she is a pearl beyond price. Let her know that you're pleased. You'll know she's good if she does the job as well or better and as fast or faster than you can, working under the most optimal conditions. Compliment her on her ability, or on how good the room looks.

If she's slow, but she's done a good job at what you asked her to do, don't give up hope. She'll probably pick up speed as she gets more used to the equipment and the house. If she's spent more time because she's done a job you didn't ask her to do, don't point out that it wasn't necessary, unless it was downright ir-relevant—like wiping the grids of your air conditioner and washing out the filter in Ivory suds. On the next room, be a bit more specific on what you want her to do, and point out some things that she needn't be bothered with. That's not to say that if she took five hours to do the bedroom and, as far as you can see, she didn't do anything special, that you don't have cause for worry. You do. Just make sure, before you dismiss her as incompetent that

1. She knows what's expected of her
2. She understands what is necessary.

If she's fast and sloppy, it is not a particularly difficult condition to cure. She may be trying to please you and get the maximum results in the minimum time. Let her know that you're more concerned with a thorough job done in areas which you make even more certain to define.

If she's slow and sloppy or stupid, you can string her along for a week or two, but if she doesn't seem to improve, get rid of her.

How to Break In a Maid for Keeps

Let's assume that you've latched onto someone who looks like she can defrost a freezer in fewer than three hours and is generally pretty good about not deluging your wooden floors with buckets of water. And you don't think that she's about to run off with your children and hold them for ransom. After a week or two of just pointing her in the right direction and telling her to leave things out if she doesn't know right away where they belong, you can begin to show her the natural resting places of some of your belongings. If you decide to hand her a special project, like washing down your walls, bear in mind that this is going to take time from her regular duties. And it will be a long, long time before she can clean out a closet for you—not until she knows your house inside out and knows whether you habitually save back issues of the *Grand Rapids Gazette and Blower*.

HOW TO FIRE A MAID

Some women spend years suffering through a lousy maid because the thought of firing her makes their blood run cold. Now there are several reasons for this:

1. You may be genuinely concerned that she will be unable to find another job and she has a family of eight to support and is putting herself through college at night.

2. You can't bear to hurt people's feelings because you're afraid then that they won't like you, and it's unbearable to think of being unloved. This is rather like the woman who goes into Tiffany's looking for a ten-dollar baby present and is persuaded by the salesman to send one for fifty dollars and doesn't want the salesman at Tiffany's to know that she can't afford fifty dollars and so spends it. Her thinking is erroneous in two ways: In the first place, the only person she's trying to impress is a sales clerk whom she will probably never see again, so why is she going out of her way to impress him? In the second place, sales clerks at Tiffany's have seen enough people so that your buying a fifty-dollar item is not going to convince them that you are one of the slightly less well known Ford sisters. They're going to know right off the bat who you are.

3. You can't bear the scene that's going to ensue when she tells you that you're not so great yourself, that she's only worked for you all these years out of pity, and that her husband who's just returned from the Marines is going to come down next week and bash your head in.

4. Bad as she is, she does lighten your load some, and the idea of breaking in a new one is more odious than can be believed.

There are several ways to handle this incredibly unpleasant situation. Most efficacious, I've found is a combination of two techniques, highly prized among those of us who can't face anything much more unpleasant than being told by our husbands that we should freshen up our lipstick. One is lying and the other is using the telephone. Let's say you've decided after a short period—say under three months—that Martha is totally unsatisfactory. So bad, in fact, that you're willing to go through the whole bother of getting another one. You call her up one night and tell her that you've broken your back and will need a full-time helper who's also a practical nurse. This presupposes knowledge on your part that (a) Martha works for some other people and cannot work for you full-time, and (b) that she is not a practical nurse. If you haven't researched this well you're in for an awfully unpleasant time.

Always, always give her severance pay (one to three weeks, depending on how long she's worked for you and how guilty you feel), and assure her of your availability for giving references. In fact, it's a good idea to send her a couple of nice letters of recommendation. If you don't know how to write one, look in an etiquette book. Basically the rule is to damn by omission, i.e., if Martha has been honest, upright, and reliable, you say so. If she never comes on time and misses two weeks out of three, you don't use the term "reliable."

To Whom It May Concern:

Martha Middlefiddle has been in my employ for three months. I have found her to be honest and of a pleasant disposition. She is an excellent housekeeper, if given careful directions. Martha has also taken care of my children on occasion and she has been excellent in this job.

Put your name and number at the bottom so the next hapless victim can call you and get the whole story.

Reasons to Fire a Maid

1. She is unreliable. That is, she shows up about half the time and when she does she's two hours late.

2. She's a lousy cleaner, even though you've given her lots of clear instructions and a period of several weeks to shape up.

3. She drinks or you have distinct suspicions that little things are unfindable.

4. She constantly regales you with her problems and you don't have any desire to be involved in the saga of her life.

Which is a sad way to end the chapter, but probably the commonest way, outside of total disappearance, with which one takes one's leave of one's maid, which we shall now do.

VII

Getting It All Together

It would be very nice if you could get your house clean through the power of positive thinking. Sigmund Freud and Norman Vincent Peale notwithstanding, however, there comes a time when you simply must employ sheer brute force to effect some change in your life style. So here we go, and I want to assure everyone who's reading this that I have attempted to make it as basic and painless as possible. Not here will you read about seven ways to use an old empty bleach container. Nevertheless, it is time to get to work.

Keep in mind that you're attempting to divorce housework from a place on which you work out your hang-ups and in attempting to set limits on it you have already

Made order in your tasks by using reality testing

Made order in your time by using scheduling.

Now creating physical order within the house makes the house no longer so threatening and guilt-provoking (in reality) but also, by being less chaotic, makes it less able to support displacement. Additionally, depending on the degree to which you identify with your house, it should make you feel a bit more ordered in your head.

It's not easy to put a house back together. In addition to the sheer physical drain, you may be fighting it all the way—not wanting to lose this means of sublimation and displacement.

This chapter is for everyone who has, over the last

month or year or five years, let the house get away from her. (Of course, the image has its attraction. Maybe, if you really tried hard, it would just collapse under the weight of its own rubble and you could collect under the Acts of God clause of your homeowner's insurance and start all over again.) What you have to do is to pull it back together. Once a room is under control in terms of organization, it's relatively simple to keep it in running order. If you can't quite face rearranging your kitchen cabinets now or in the near future, you can at least keep things from getting worse by employing what we are calling:

CREATIVE DISPLACEMENT

Once upon a time, when the world was new, when you first got married, or right after you moved, or when the painters came and painted, everything was in order. But, life being what it is, you started throwing your bracelets into the top drawer of your dresser because you didn't feel like getting the jewelry box out of the bottom drawer because it was something else to do. Or you started stacking plates from different sets of china together. Or maybe the bookshelves are studded with old wedding invitations, pieces of broken pottery that you've been meaning to mend, and the umbrella cover that belonged to the umbrella that's lying broken in the bottom of the hall closet somewhere. It has been a long time since you have been able to find the little gold bracelet; your favorite kitchen knife is missing in action, and you weren't able to find your son's Little League uniform and he is not speaking to you ever again. In other words, total chaos. (Putting things in the wrong place is the first step in creating chaos. Feedback from chaos can go straight to your head depending on the degree of identification you have with your house.)

Terminal disorganization is difficult to cure, but it can often be arrested, and kept from spreading, by applying Creative Displacement. (This sounds very professional and I dare say there's probably a nice vivid scatological phrase that would do as well or better. However, this is a book meant for family consumption.)

It might be valid to differentiate between *Haut Debris* and *Debris en Bas*—or what you need to keep and put in the wrong place and what you should have tossed in the garbage when the thought crossed your mind. If you sometimes think there is a certain superfluity of objects in your home, like the extra tire from the '43 Dodge that has been on top of your washing machine for five years, or the old air conditioner filters you've been saving because you're sure you read somewhere that they could be used as insulation if the refrigerator ever gave out, you might ponder your reason for keeping unnecessary things:

1. It may represent something else. Maybe the tire comes from the car your family had when you were two years old and you like the tire because it reminds you of your happy childhood.

2. Maybe possessing objects makes you feel secure. Perhaps you identify strongly with objects and feel you're symbolically throwing yourself out.

3. Perhaps you feel disoriented and feel objects are a tie between the past and the future.

4. Possibly you have a need to fill all empty spaces representing a need to combat feelings of emptiness in your life.

(All this goes to show how far out you can get if you try to analyze absolutely everything. There are other ways to satisfy your anal drives—you could start an organized collection of things, like matchbook covers or old tires from '43 Dodges. On the other hand, if throwing things gets you uptight, you might as well keep them until they threaten to take over your house.)

Beginning NOW, you have to set aside some place, depending on the size of your house and the number of movable objects, for the sole purpose of collecting things that are found where they don't belong. From now on you have to flout the temptation to throw something in the general direction of its proper place, and toss it instead into the Debris Depot. This has the double virtue of saving time and energy expended in putting things back in their place several times a day, since it's much faster and the house looks just as neat. It also prevents disorganization from spreading any further. The space that you set aside can be anything from one drawer in a tiny apartment, to a drawer in every room and two closets in a large house. Experiment. But make sure you don't have to walk more than several steps to put it away.

The catch to this clever little idea is that you must, absolutely without fail, spend one hour a week putting things back where they belong with absolutely no cheating. (This is the explanation for the mysterious "D.O." which stands for "Displacement Order" and which you all thought had something to do with deodorizing your dog, that's listed as a once-a-week job.)

Having sworn to uphold the principle of Creative Displacement as the only road to salvation, you are now ready to embark on the odious task of putting the pieces of your house back together. I suggest starting in the living room, since it's probably the least disorganized room of the house, which seems as good a reason as any.

How to Organize the Living Room

1. Get two big boxes. Go around the room and divide anything that's not in its place between the two boxes. One is for things that belong in the living room.

The other is for things that don't belong in the living room. Sort through all the drawers, cabinets, and closets this way. If you don't have enough room in the boxes, use the middle of the floor. Don't do any cleaning whatsoever while you're doing this. That means if the dust is two inches thick on the bottom of your record cabinet, ignore it utterly. Its time will come.

2. Take the carton that holds the things that don't belong in the living room and put them in the bottom of a closet somewhere. Don't spend any time sorting through them. Unless you find your engagement ring which you lost three months ago, in which case you may put it on.

3. Take a good long look at the space that's available to you for putting things away in the living room. If you're going to have to stuff drawers and cabinets, you'll have to weed out. If you don't know how to weed out, do something like this:

A. Look through the pile of living room stuff and remove anything you haven't missed, or haven't used, or is broken and beyond repair.

B. Put all that in yet another carton.

C. Keep doing that until you're down to what will comfortably fit.

4. Put away neatly where it belongs what's left for the living room.

5. Bookshelves and

6. Record shelves

You should know by now exactly what state of organization is necessary to maintain sanity around your house. If it's enough that the books are standing up straight and the records are not lying at horizontal angles across the arm of your sofa, fix it that way. On the other hand, you may find it vital that the books be arranged by subject and cross-referenced by author and title. Or you may be like a friend I once had who used to carry books around according to what she was wearing—a light green copy of *Ulysses* when she wore green; a slim dark-blue volume of Keats when she dressed in blue, and so on. She didn't get very many books finished, but she did have a reputation for being awfully well turned out.

7. Try to set the room up for convenience. If cocktail napkins and coasters have been languishing in a drawer by the record cabinet put them in the drawer by the coffee table. On the other hand, if the extra phonograph needle is in an end-table drawer, put it in the space the coasters took up.

8. If there are magazines lying around, grit your teeth and throw them out. Unless you have the complete set of *Ramparts* from the first issue, it's unlikely they will ever be worth much. If you have vague notions of keeping magazines around for your children to use in lavishly illustrated sixth-grade reports five years from now, stick them in a box and tuck them away in the attic.

9. Take a paper and pencil and make a list of any repairs that have to be made. Then, taking into consideration the priorities you've established, list the major jobs that have to be done in the living room. Your list might look something like this:

Repairs
1. Get ring off coffee table
2. Put drawer pull back on drawer
3. Get new lampshade
4. Fix ripped seam in sofa cushion

Major Cleaning
1. Get spots off rug
2. Get spots off sofa
3. Wash all the woodwork

How to Organize the Bedroom, Dining Room, Family Room, Children's Room

For all of these rooms, follow the plan for the living room. Of course there'll be variations. For instance, in the kids' rooms, if any, you ought to spend a good amount of time reassessing the toy situation. I know a little boy of five whose room was overflowing with toys, but his mother always complained that he was constantly in the kitchen bugging her about what to play with. When she finally decided one day to take a good long look at his toys she found that he'd outgrown twenty percent of them; ten percent were useless because they were missing half of their pieces; ten percent were broken or without batteries; fifteen percent were too old for him and he didn't know what to do with them; and twenty percent were okay but out of his reach. What it came down to was he had a nice set of building blocks and a whole lot of colored paper. So first make sure that you weed out what's useless and second, remember that if the sewing cards are three feet up in the closet, it's not too likely he's going to get them down and play with them.

In the dining room, if there is one, try to avoid having tablecloths that are used twice a year in drawer space that could be devoted to placemats, napkins, or silver that's used at the table and stored in the kitchen. Reality test!

Closets and Drawers

The biggest problem you're going to have in any room is the problem of closets and drawers. Do each closet one by one, and do all the drawers in any cabinet at one time. When you're taking things out of any one closet or set of drawers, be sure you separate things out into the same two piles—things that belong and things that don't. And put them away. Stuff them in. Don't even try to put them back where they belong. A lot of the problem of closets and drawers has to do with their total insufficiency to hold the things they're meant to. When you're putting things back, you might keep in mind the following possible space-saving aids.

If your husband doesn't have a tie rack, get him one.

If you're storing shoes in boxes, switch to shoebags.

If you're plagued with nightgowns that slide off hangers, twist up the ends of the hangers.

Stick a few shower curtain hooks over the rods of your closet to hold belts or buy belt rings.

If you have a very high closet, install a rod at the very top of it and hang your out of season or seldom used clothes there.

Store extra blankets between the mattress and the box spring of the bed.

Hang a shoebag, which you can get in the dime store for about a dollar, on the back of every closet door. Use it for gloves, scarves, chain belts, change purses, sunglasses—all the things that tend to get mixed up in your dresser drawers.

In children's closets, install a second rod, lower than the original one. This has the double benefit of adding storage space and making clothes low enough for small children to reach.

If your clothes have a tendency to fall together, you can cut notches in the clothes pole about 3″ apart. Or you can buy things that fit over the rods and have slots in them to stick the hangers on.

By the way, it's a good idea to clean closets when you're angry, since there's a better chance that you'll throw things out in anger that you might hold onto in a better mood. It may be because you're displacing the hostility that's surfacing onto objects you've endowed with your fantasies. This makes a lot of sense when you're throwing out old love letters (hopefully not from your husband).

You will get the best cleaning results, obviously, if you clean out the closet of the person you're feeling the least kindly toward—but how can you be sure? Psychiatry as applied to closet cleaning is not one of our more exact sciences.

Drawers

Follow the ground rules for sorting out closets when you're sorting out drawers. If in doubt, throw it out. One very general rule for storing things in drawers: if a lot has to go into them, make use of dividers (cheap clear plastic vegetable boxes are good for holding all your cosmetics or all your gloves or all your old jewelry). If the drawers are relatively uncrowded, don't use dividers or separators since they just clutter the drawers unnecessarily.

If your drawers are insufferably crowded, consider the possibility of underbed storage chests, which are sold in notions departments and dime stores. They're useful for storing sweaters in summer and bathing suits in winter, but they're useless for storing things to which easy access is required. One exception to that rule might be a child's room with limited toy storage space. If you have an old dresser drawer, or can get hold of a strong carton and cut down the top to fit under the child's bed, you can put the used but less popular toys in there and pull them out for play. If you have blocks and no block cart, you might consider that as a possibility. Or if your child has a collection of 1,023 tin cars he refuses to part with. Use your discretion.

Organizing the Bathroom

1. It's not too likely that there's too much debris in the bathroom, but if there is, deal with it in the same way as with the other rooms.

2. If there's space for it, keep the cleaning stuff you need for the bathroom somewhere in it. You may have a cabinet under the sink, or there might be space behind the curtains for sponges, Ajax, Vanish, Windex, and a roll of paper towels.

3. The medicine chest: Most people keep all the wrong things in their medicine chest—the stuff that George took last winter when he had that terrible rash. An ancient bottle of blood-red nailpolish; prenatal vitamins that you took when you were pregnant with your six-year-old. So

A. Throw out all the prescription medicine. It's conceivably a danger from old age when it's been there a year and it's more probably a danger when you use George's medicine on Susie's rash which turns out to be not nearly the same thing and makes her break out in blue spots.

B. The medicine chest should be used primarily for things that are used in the bathroom—razors and blades, toothpaste and toothbrushes, shampoo, face creams, and so forth. But it's probably not necessary to have the three toothbrushes you used before this one and four small tubes of Gleam toothpaste samples that you never would use since you're a devoted Crest toothpaste user.

C. The second purpose of the medicine chest—and if there isn't enough room this can be transferred bodily to the kitchen or to a shelf in the linen closet—as long as it's all together and can be gotten at—is emergency first aid. You should have on hand

iodine or Merthiolate
boric acid

pHisoHex or tincture of green soap for cleaning
 wounds

a tweezers and a needle for taking out splinters

(you could stick the needle in a cork, if you were so
 minded, and then you'd be able to find it) and a
 pack of matches to sterilize the needle

oral and rectal thermometers and Vaseline if you
 have children

whatever you take for a headache or for an upset
 stomach

Band Aids

gauze and adhesive tape for large cuts

D. The third and last purpose for a medicine chest
is to store medicine, which goes to show the essential
absurdity of language (who, come to think of it, ever
puts gloves in the glove compartment?). Most people
stuff the thing up not only with the pills of yesteryear,
but with all the patent medicines that they take every
few months. Unless your medicine chest can take a
whole lot of stuff, get yourself a plastic box (we are
very big on plastic boxes in our house) and put in it
all those things like Sucrets, and Coricidin, and the four
different varieties of cough medicine, and the Sominex
you take every time you've stayed up the night before
on No-doz. When you're sick and you need medicine,
go to the sick box. And it will be there instead of being
hidden behind the shaving cream.

How to Organize a Kitchen

Kitchens tend to become repositories for debris without even trying. (Either because it's about the most
emotionally loaded room in the house next to the bedroom—or maybe even more so since it's the dispensary
of love to the whole family. And the objects you have
here are the most likely to be your *own* thing.) So first
of all, clear it out and shove the displaced objects in
with the other stuff you've collected. Then prepare to

meet the worst job of all, which is creating an island of peace and harmony out of what was probably rank chaos. All it takes is a little attention, intelligence, and the will power of a child who has discovered where his Christmas presents are hidden and doesn't peek, to clean out your cabinets and drawers and start all over again on a new and higher plane.

There are, when you come to think of it, three centers in the kitchen:

Preparation
Cooking
Cleaning

Or, if you prefer, where you throw it together, where you throw it at them, and where you mop it up. Ideally, the three centers should describe a triangle of stove, sink and refrigerator, although they seldom do. If you can manage it:

Each appliance should have a counter alongside it.

The refrigerator door should open out so when it's opened the door is not between it and the counter on which you're preparing food.

The dishwasher, should you have one, should be directly next to the sink.

At any rate, one of the biggest kitchen problems is the lack of sufficient space to store food, drink, and the staff of life, alcohol, let alone six-packs of bubblegum for emergencies. (Women who buy a lot may not be merely efficient. What might they really be afraid of running out of? Consider the equation between kitchen and love. On the other hand, women who are always running out may be expressing an unwillingness to mete out love. Or maybe it's security? Oh, well.) The following sneaky little devices might give you little more room to move around in.

More Counter Space*

You could install a chopping block on top of the dishwasher, assuming you have one, assuming it's a convenient place to chop things.

You could get your toaster, blender, and mixer off the counter and onto the wall by putting up little 12-by 8-inch shelves, if there's space on the walls.

You could put up a pegboard, which has the dual attraction of making everything visible and getting lots of stuff out of the drawers.

If you have a narrow little hall that's good for nothing, you could put up narrow long shelves to serve as a pantry.

If you don't have them already, you could get and put up a utensil rack, a spice rack, a towel rack, and a knife rack, thereby getting even more out of the drawers and cabinets. Of course your walls are beginning to look a little cluttered.

You could investigate those new little plastic drawers that fit onto the wall under the cabinets.

You could go to the hardware store and take a look at some of Rubbermaid's space-saving devices. For instance, you might have a shelf that's eighteen inches high. They have a little plastic thing with feet that sits inside and makes another shelf. Very good for storing twice as many soups. (You can also do this with bricks and board.) Also, lazy susans, with two or three tiers, not only increase the cubic inches of storage but make things much easier to get at.

---

* You may not want it. Some people want everything where they can get at it. Some people want everything shut away. Catching on?

Cabinets

You might as well clean them, since you're going to take everything out of them anyway. To clean them, you'll need a pail, some household cleaner, a bit of steel wool for where the spills that never got picked up welded themselves to the shelf, and a few rags or a sponge. Put on those rubber gloves and make the solution strong.

Don't do the cabinets one at a time and just put the same old crap back in a different order. In this case, where everything is going to be moved, you might look at the groupings on the next page and get yourself some big cardboard boxes to hold things. If there's shelf paper down, tear it up. Contact can stay, as long as it's not beyond repair. Really, do put down Contact, or paint the insides of your cabinets something other than dead white which looks dirtier faster than anything else. Wash the cabinets out and dry them with one of the rags. If you've got a bug problem, now's the time to go into the cabinets with the strongest stuff you can tolerate. As you take things out of your cabinets and especially out of your drawers, make a separate pile of things you can't remember when you used last. Have a moment of truth. Give the middle-sized wire whisk to a needy friend. The thing is to keep cabinets as uncrowded as possible. Look into the possibility of storing things on high shelves, if you don't use them much.

The Sink

Put under the sink or nearby only your kitchen cleaners. Other cleaning supplies should have a home of their own, if possible.

mild soap or detergent for dishes
sponges

steel wool pads, if you use them

scouring powder

towels and dishcloths (on a rack, really)

dishwasher detergent (if you have one)

vegetable brush (because you scrub your vegetables, if you do, over the sink)

a spatula for scraping dishes (if you do—I use my hands or a fork)

garbage pail (because most of the garbage comes to the sink)

rubber gloves

hand lotion (an optional long-term proposition—of course you should, but how many people do?)

colanders and strainers (because you drain things into the sink)

Above the sink or dishwasher, should it work out that way, or nearby, put:

dishes and glasses (the ones you use most if there's not room for all)

The Stove

burn ointment (Why go all the way to the bathroom? How many times have you burned yourself in the bathroom?)

big box of baking soda (if you still haven't gotten a fire extinguisher)

pots and pans and covers

cooking thermometers

ladles

serving spoons

potato masher

coffee, tea, hot chocolate (because it's close to the source of hot water)

hot cereals

crackers (if you serve them with soup)

gravy mixes (the kind that go directly into the pot)

meat sauces (ditto)

bouillon cubes (ditto)

a big salt shaker full of flour for thickening sauces

whatever you tend to stick on top of things—toasted almonds, croutons, crystallized violets

salt and pepper

Near the Refrigerator

On the counter (or higher up, if you can, on a shelf):

mixer

blender

cutting board (if it slips a lot, put two rubber bands around the ends)

cannisters (flour, sugar, whatever)

In drawers or on a pegboard:

egg beater

graters

scissors

utility knives

bottle openers

can openers

spatula

mixing spoons

measuring cups

measuring spoons

In the cabinet below:

cake pans and cookie sheets

casseroles

salad bowls

onions and potatoes (unless you have a bug problem)

In the cabinet above:

staples

canned goods

Then there will be:

a drawer for silverware

a messy drawer

aluminum foil and plastic wrap or bags or waxpaper

or whatever you wrap things in in a dispenser or a drawer.

In putting things in their proper place, remember a few ground rules:

It's easier to reach up than down, so put your most used things at eye level.

If you only use good china, glasses, silver, etc., to entertain, make a separate area for them, one that's out of the way.

Obviously, use your discretion. I doubt that anyone uses or has all of the things listed. And some kitchens don't lend themselves terribly well to any kind of organization beyond keeping the pepper within hailing distance of the salt. If you don't bake very much you'd hardly want to have all those baking things in such a place of honor. Just try to think of your equipment in terms of the area it services and file it accordingly.

Try hanging your paper towel dispenser near the stove rather than over the sink. You'll use a lot fewer paper towels which is (a) cheaper, and (b) ecologically sound if you use a towel for wiping your hands and a paper towel for draining things on and maybe wiping up spills.

Try to have a stool in the kitchen, one that moves around easily. You can get used to sitting down while you do things.

If your washing machine or dryer are in the kitchen, then obviously your soaps, bleaches, powders, and potions should be there, too.

Presumably the house is now in order. Filthy, but in order. You have perhaps been wondering if we would ever get around to how to clean things, or whether somehow we would fastidiously avoid the subject of dirt. We are merely working up to it in easy stages.

VIII

Understanding Filth

Dirt, as any college freshman knows, is threatening, but the inability to deal with it through ignorance can be another cause of disorder. If you don't know how to do something, you leave yourself wide open to a plethora of wrong ways to do it, making the tendency to disorder that much stronger. So in this chapter we'll begin by explaining just exactly what dirt is, why things get dirty, how you have to clean them when they get dirty, and why you should bother cleaning them when they get dirty.

The first thing that you should be aware of is that you're dealing with the three discrete and separate forms of dirt in your house. The first we've discussed at some length—that's displaced objects or clutter. (Take for instance the philosophical question of the angels dancing on the head of a pin. The angels are not making the head of the pin dirty, they're making it cluttered.) To get rid of dirt that's clutter all you need to replace the object in its proper place and make it stop being dirt is your hands, with the addition perhaps of a shovel if things are really bad.

The second kind of dirt is dust, or soot, or anything that gently drifts from out of the air onto the table. Dust is the simplest kind of dirt to get rid of and could almost be called preventive cleaning. All you have to do is brush it away with a rag, vacuum cleaner, or brush of some kind. If you don't get rid of it, it turns into the third kind of dirt, which is grime.

When dust combines with moisture of one kind or another, it can no longer be removed by purely physical means, since it has, in effect, gone into solution. Take a windowsill—if you don't dust it for a long time, some of the dust combines with moisture in the air to produce grime. Then to get it off, you have to put it into solution, or dilute it with water or another fluid to remove it. As we will see, dust not removed reasonably promptly turns into something else. Or worse.

If you never get the dust off your sofa, eventually it will begin to discolor or even fall apart. Or take finger-prints, for instance, of which one must generally take a lot. Because dust wasn't removed from the fingers, it combined with the grease in the fingers, and to remove the smudgy decorations from the wall you have to re-move both the dust and the grease by chemical means. To remove any dust that's gone into combination with grease, or to remove grease alone, requires something more than water, since as you know oil (grease) and water don't mix. What you need is soap, which emul-sifies dirt and grease, that is, it surrounds the offending material with a film allowing it to come loose from the surface on which it rests, to be sloshed off into the water. I use the word soap here, although you may read detergent, since it has the same emulsifying effect. If this is all too scientific for you, we will leave it for a while until we get into the chapter on potions.

The fourth way that things get dirty is when a thing that is not dirt by itself gets displaced. Grape juice isn't dirt until it lands on your white rug. Axle grease is perfectly acceptable in the crank case of the car, or wherever it sits in the car, but when it gets tracked onto your kitchen floor it's dirt. Cookie crumbs on the floor are another example. So anything that's in the wrong place at the wrong time and can't be picked up and put back where it belongs is displaced dirt. If it can be picked up and put back, then it's clutter. But for the purposes of this discussion we will lump cookie-crumb type dirt in with dust and staining-type dirt with grime since they are treated identically.

So, as you march purposefully around your house, you should be aware of the different kinds of dirt.

1. Clutter
2. Dust (or other particles that can be removed without resorting to chemical means)
3. Grime (or things that have to be removed by resorting to chemical means)

That the second often turns into the third and becomes harder to remove is somehow parallel to one's experiences with living—that the longer you let a thing go, the harder it is to do. Unless, of course, it disappears, which unfortunately is not the case with dirt.

It's all so simple it's a wonder nobody's ever thought of it before. Well, actually, loads of people have, beginning with the cavewoman who got the idea of sticking some branches together to get up the mess on the floor, all the way down to the giant soap companies who discovered that there were at least three thousand variations on the theme of soap. Because you should be able to see that the only difference between a cleaning closet that contains a rag and a bar of soap and a cleaning closet that has fourteen different appliances and all the latest, newer, faster-working, guaranteed to make you get through your job in half the time potions is the amount of manual labor that you have to expend. When they talk about removing the drudgery from housework that's what they're talking about. Somewhere between my friend Ann, the ecology freak, who is trying to reduce things back to a rag, a broom, and a bar of 99 and 44/100 percent pure Ivory soap and the consumer about whom the soap giants' marketing directors dream every night, there lies an elusive medium.

Tools That You Need for Getting Rid of Dust

vacuum cleaner and attachments
carpet sweeper (optional)
broom
dust mop (optional)
feather duster (optional)
dustpan and brush
rags

Tools That You Need for Getting Rid of Grime

a pail
rags
paper towels (optional)
sponges (optional)
wet mop (optional)
an art gum eraser (optional)

Tools That You Need for Getting Rid of Dust and Grime That Don't Seem to Fit into Either of the Above Categories

a step stool
rubber gloves

Two Optional Tools That We Will Discuss in Their Place

a wax applicator
a floor buffer

Obviously, you *can* get along without most of the list, which is the reason for (optional).

And now that you understand dirt, it should make it easier to understand the tools that are required to deal with it. Tools used without chemical helpers are used almost without exception to dispose of dust.

A VACUUM CLEANER

Of all the cleaning tools, the vacuum cleaner is virtually the only one that couldn't be bought with a book or two of trading stamps, when people used them. Prices range to up over a hundred dollars, so it's actually a good-sized investment and you should know a little about them before you get out and buy them. It used to be that a woman got a vacuum cleaner when she got married and when her daughter got married the mother passed on the old one and blew herself to a new one. The way it goes now, you're lucky if a vacuum cleaner lasts a good five years.

There are two varieties of vacuum cleaner and each has, as might be expected, its advantages and disadvantages. There's the cannister type and then there's the upright.

Cannister Type
More convenient for above the floor cleaning
Better for above the floor cleaning
Are generally cheaper
Are easier to carry
Can clean more easily under furniture

Upright Models
Are better for cleaning rugs and carpets; they get out embedded dirt.

Can be purchased with attachments but generally the suction on the attachments is not as high as the cannister type.

In other words, if you have a lot of rugs or deep carpets, the upright will do a better job for you. The cannister type carpet cleaning attachment will eventually get out just about as much dirt as the upright, but it will take a much longer time doing it. If rugs and carpets aren't a particular problem you're probably better off with a cannister type—it's considerably more versatile.

Whatever kind of vacuum you use, don't vacuum up large pieces of paper or string; they clog up the hose. If your hose does get clogged (you'll know because the suction is less or nonexistent) straighten out a wire coat hanger and poke around. Be careful not to stick the wire through the hose, while you're about it, but if you do that you can patch it up well enough with adhesive tape or friction tape to finish up for the day. If the wire coat hanger doesn't do the trick, hook the hose up to the blower and, being careful to point the hose toward someplace where you don't mind having a pile of dirt land, turn it on. If that doesn't work, take the rotten, sullen machine to the vacuum cleaner repair shop and pay for your carelessness.

You really ought to stick a magnet on the front of the cleaner to pick up pins and campaign buttons and other small metallic objects that can work their way into the motor and wreak havoc.

Check the bag and try to see to it that it doesn't get too full. An overflowing bag lowers the suction and removing an overflowing bag is way up there in the stellar galaxy of jobs I would like to see Pat Nixon doing.

By the way, the blower attachment is handy for getting to places you can't get to with the floor attachment. Just turn it on and blow the dust out to where you can get at it.

If you are supersensitive to smells, you can drip a little oil of cinnamon into the bag when you put in a new one, and your house will smell as though you've been baking apple pies in the bedroom. Which is fine, if you want people to think you've been baking pies in the bedroom.

One more thing in buying a vacuum: horsepower is

no index to suction. And neither high power nor high suction alone is sufficient to clean carpets. So shop around, check current Consumer's Union reports, and don't buy from the door-to-door salesman whose little razzler dazzler beats as it sweeps as it cleans, then dies as he flies out of town.

Vacuum cleaner brushes wear out eventually, so if your cleaning results are not up to par, and if the bag is empty and the suction seems about right, take a look and see if the brushes look worn down. They can be lowered at the repair store.

In addition to the standard kind of vacuum cleaner we just described, there are lighter and heavier kinds, too. Light weight vacuum cleaners are sort of in between carpet sweepers and vacuums, and I can't for the life of me imagine why anyone would want to spend any money on them, but then, you never know where some people get their kicks. They're okay for cleaning floors and getting the topsoil off rugs, but they lack sufficient suction to be worth much on upholstery or draperies or walls or whatever you use your vacuum cleaner for.

Heavy Duty Cleaners—sometimes called shop vacuums—are essentially all suction and a lot of it without any frills. It's the sort of handy dandy extra gadget that might be for you if you're fanatical about cleaning up your patio or if your husband regularly carpets the basement in a shower of wood shavings. Even though the suction is high, it's no substitute for a regular model, being clumsy, rough on the furniture it bumps against, and poorly endowed with attachments.

Vacuum Cleaner Attachments

The long one with a brush is for vacuuming up floors.

The long one without a brush is for vacuuming up rugs and carpets.

The short one without a brush is for vacuuming upholstery and draperies and curtains.

The short one with a brush is for vacuuming woodwork and walls and ceilings and maybe wood furniture if you have any that looks like it might respond to vacuuming rather than dusting.

The long skinny one that comes to a point on the end is for vacuuming into the cracks behind sofa cushions and into any other hard to get to places.

Then there are all sorts of other vacuum cleaner attachments, ranging from paint sprayers to atom smashers. However, the only ones we're going to deal with in this book are the ones listed above. If you happen to have lost one or more, you can, of course, substitute, using brush for brush—however, it just makes the job a little harder.

CARPET SWEEPER

Carpet sweepers are the only alternative to vacuum cleaners (assuming you find it inconvenient to beat with your hands or use a broom) for getting crud off rugs and, strangely enough, carpets. A lot of women like them for what is euphemistically called "hitting the middle." I find them a nuisance, personally. Also they go wrong and don't pick up dirt as much as they spread around what was left in their insides the last time. But then, perhaps I'm prejudiced. Maybe I had a bad experience with carpet sweepers in my formative years. If you do have, or get, a carpet sweeper, there are a few helpful things to know about it:

1. If you run a damp paper towel over the brushes, it will pick up the dust and dirt better.

2. Keep it emptied, but keep it clean also. Clip the threads that collect in the brushes with scissors before pulling them out or sucking them out with a vacuum. If they still look dirty to you, you can soak them in a

solution of household cleaner, rinse them well, and dry them out of the sun.

There is one kind of carpet sweeper that I unhesitatingly recommend. Do invest four or five bucks in a toy carpet sweeper which is tiny, will fit anywhere, and serves nearly quite as well as a big one. It's marvelous for picking up the contents of a spilled ashtray. It is altogether one of the neatest things for battling dirt and it has an added advantage: children love to use it and they do it for such long periods of time that they do quite a creditable job. While you're at it, you might pick up a child's mop, which is just the right size for getting into the corners where the ceilings meet the walls, should you have any need to get into the corners where the ceilings meet the walls.

THE BROOM

Although I admit the possibility of people who don't know how to boil an egg, I find it hard to credit someone over the age of three not knowing how to sweep with a broom. It may indeed, like the ability to blink your eyes without anyone ever telling you how, be a genetic trait. Brooms sweep up loose dirt on floors that aren't waxed or carpeted. There is probably some time and motion study somewhere about the most efficient way to sweep, and some orthopedic surgeon has probably delivered a long paper on the proper way to hold a broom in order to minimize backstrain, but you can't go too far wrong here.

The best kind of brooms, I understand, are made of tampico fibers. A broom has passed its prime when it keeps losing its bristles, at which point you throw it out, or stick it in the garage for a garage broom or, if you can't tolerate waste, become a witch and use it for your equipment. Ideally, a broom shouldn't be stood on the floor when it's being stored, but hung by that little loop on the top of it. If you feel constrained to clean it, the best way is to kill two birds with one broom, as it were, and use it to clean out your bathtub. You fill the tub with detergent and hot water and scrub the sides with the broom, or the broom with the sides, depending on how you look at it. If you never cleaned your broom, I bet nobody would complain. I don't clean mine and I doubt it's made of tampico fiber, either.

Of course, you don't really need a broom; you could get down on your knees and use a rag. But in keeping house you need all the help you can get, and I think even the most minimal housekeeper should have a broom in her broom closet. (I hate to keep hedging, but it's possible that your entire house is carpeted, in which case you could do without.)

A DUST MOP

There's really nothing a dust mop can do that a broom with a rag tied around it can't. Essentially it's a rag on a stick, to save you bending and reaching. You need a dust mop (or a rag on a broom, if you like) for wood floors. Wood floors can't be mopped with a wet mop (the water would damage the wood) and sweeping with a broom not only scratches the finish on a fine wood floor, but doesn't pick up the dust that settles on a waxed surface. Essentially, when you use a dust mop, you're dusting the floor. When you dust mop the floor, try to do it with the grain, rather than with a circular motion. If you're not satisfied with the way your dust mop is picking up dust, you can buy in a hardware store, or a dime store, a dust mop cover that is specially treated cloth with a somewhat sticky surface that picks up dust.

When you buy a dust mop, just make sure you can remove it from the handle, so that you can clean it. A light mop will be easier to move around, and one made of synthetic fibers is slightly preferable to one made of cotton. Dust mops need to be cleaned when they get dirty, because they won't pick up dust if they're clogged with it. You can clean a dust mop in more ways than you need to know: Shaking it or turning the vacuum cleaner on it will remove the clumps of dust. To get the dirt out that's been ground in, you can throw it in the washing machine.

THE FEATHER DUSTER

I will go out on a limb and say that I think a feather duster is an absolute necessity, especially for crash cleaning, since nothing gets dust off things quite so fast. Mostly, it scatters the dust onto the floor, but that's what you have a dust mop for. Feather dusting is a symptomatic measure with no permanence. However, it's four times as fast as cleaning with a dustcloth, especially on non-flat areas like telephones and candles, and potted palms. There is probably some sort of advantage in having an expensive feather duster made out of Himalayan left-footed ostriches or something, but it seems to me that the only guide is to shake it in the store to see if many feathers come out and if they do, to look knowingly down your nose at the salesman and ask to see another. And buy the biggest and prettiest one that you can afford. There is something quite earnest and charming about the sight of a woman wielding a feather duster. It has a certain *je ne sais quoi* —a look of genteel hard work.

Shake the old duster out and, should you ever want to wash it—which you might if you perennially whip it over a table that has strawberry jam sticking to it, roll up your sleeves and do this: Fill the sink with lukewarm water and a mild detergent like Ivory Liquid. Get it very sudsy. Dip the duster down through the suds, swish it swiftly through the water and lift it out. Refill the sink with clear lukewarm water. Swish it around a little. Then do the suds bit all over again and add maybe ¼ cup of vinegar to the rinse water. Finish up shaking it out and letting it dry, feather side hanging listlessly down, out of the sun.

THE WHISK BROOM

It hadn't occurred to me until quite recently that a whisk broom was just as good if not better and a whole lot easier for vacuuming upholstery than a vacuum cleaner attachment down in the back of the closet somewhere. A good whisk broom can also be used for getting into the 4,323 crevices and cracks that your vacuum, mop, or broom won't get into on that day you decide you simply have to get into them.

I don't think there's very much variation in whisk broom quality, but I suggest you tug gently at the bristles or whiskers or broomlets, whatever they're called, before you buy. When you use it to clean upholstery, whisk it over the surface hard enough so that you can see some dust rise. Using a follow-through, of course, so the dust doesn't settle right back in. Should you wish to clean it, swish it around in warm water and mild soap and rinse it in clear cold water. Hang it with the bristles down.

DUSTPAN AND BRUSH

Come to think of it, you don't need a dustpan and brush either. You could pick up the big pieces with your hands and get the rest with a rag. But what the hell, unless you buy plastic and leave it by your kitchen wastebasket the night a fire starts because you threw in a batch of oily rags, a dustpan should last you through your marriage. And divorce statistics being what they are, there's about a one in three chance that it will outlast your marriage. (In California, you should average one dustpan every two marriages. It's nice to know that some things endure.)

You use a dustpan to collect the stuff that you swept up with the broom. There is a real division between the long-handled dustpan ladies and the short-handled dustpan ladies. The long-handled ones say theirs is better because you don't have to stoop. You just sweep the crud in with your broom. The short-handled ladies feel that a broom does not get all the stuff off the floor and into the dustpan and since there is no long-handled dustpan brush, they stick to the short one. Personally, I am a short-handled dustpan lady, probably because my family have been short-handled dustpan ladies for several generations. I also like the old metal kind with the rubber rim somewhat better, possibly because of the way I got burned but also because the new plastic kinds, although their design is worthy of inclusion in the Museum of Modern Art permanent collections, do tend to warp, and when you brush the dirt in, it gets underneath and it's back to the old hand and damp rag method until you get around to buying another one.

One little tip, if you run a damp rag over the dustpan or wet your hands and shake them over it, the dust won't blow out of it when you carry it to the wastebasket to empty it. As for cleaning it every once in a while, like during eclipses of the sun, you might wipe the pan with a damp sponge and shake the brush out into your back yard.

RAGS

Come let us visit that most misunderstood and least known area of cleaning tools, the lowly rag.

If you're ever stumped for a shower present, you could do worse than to bale up a bunch of your extra rags, tie a pretty ribbon around them and give them to a bride-to-be. Because brides-to-be, for all they begin housekeeping with, start out lacking in old diapers, torn sheets, hopelessly stained shirts, and worn-out tea towels. Basically you need two kinds of rag:

1. The kind you want to soak up a lot of fluid, so you can use it for scrubbing walls or floors or what have you. Rags in this category are really rags—whatever you have around—although knitted cotton, like old undershirts, dishtowels, diapers, and the like, will do the best.

2. The high-class rag, the one you use for dusting and polishing. Since you're dusting, you don't want a rag that will give out more dust, so you need a lintless cloth. The best kind to use you actually have to go out and buy, and the idea of buying a rag may sound sacrilegious to some. However, the fact is that nothing beats cheesecloth for dusting and polishing. If you feel that buying a rag is ridiculous—that they should be created out of discarded things—your next best bets are:

soft wool (the static electricity it generates gets up dust very effectively)

lintless cotton: very old and worn diapers and undershirts will serve.

One warning on rags. It's very easy to become a rag collector. You need no more than a dozen at the outside. In fact, a dozen diapers and a couple of wads of cheesecloth should last anyone for a year or two. Many of you may remember that large laundry bag full of rags in our homes as children. Remember, many of your parents grew up in the Depression and conceived a horror of wasting anything. Has it ever occurred to you that the bottom seven-eighths of that bag probably stood from year to year taking up space and breeding strange and unknown organisms dropped in spoors from outer space? I have no suggestion for what to do with superfluous rags if you happen to be glutted with them. But they are superfluous, so give them to a friend or use them to make a tail for a kite or throw them out.

WHAT ABOUT PAPER TOWELS AND SPONGES?

Well, what about them? They're as good as rags for some things, and they do have the advantage of being disposable (I find the whole idea of reusable paper towels unspeakably depressing). True you don't have to wash them, but they do cost more money than rags, and except for quick wipe-up jobs they don't do as well.

It is the sort of decision you must make after long communion with your soul. I have a friend who could easily afford to switch entirely to paper towels, but feels it's somehow immoral not to have a rag bag. So she *has* a rag bag and uses paper towels.

Sponges, however, do have their place. One place they have is by the sink and the bathtub, where they look infinitely nicer than a smelly old dishcloth. Sponges come in two varieties: real, the kind that come from the sea, and fake plastic ones that come in decorator colors. The real ones are cheaper, last longer, and, if they don't look quite so spiffy when they're new, they are rather more esthetic than the superannuated sponge that seems to hang around sinks until it develops a little smell of its own. If you opt for natural sponges, it's more economical, surprisingly enough, to buy them in smaller sizes—since they're real, they're not uniform in size and apparently it's harder to find a big piece of sponge wherever it is that sponge divers dive for them. Natural sponges should be washed from time to time in lukewarm soap suds and dried in the sun, if that's possible. Synthetic sponges look pretty and fade fast. If you're determined to keep them going as long as possible, add them to your next rag laundry and use bleach, but don't put them in the dryer. Sponges, by the way, are the medium of choice for applying thick suds, like when you clean upholstery.

A PAIL

What, after all, can one say about pails? A pail is to put water and perhaps soap into. And maybe a mop and maybe a rag. Plastic is lighter than metal, and probably the better bet. There's absolutely no reason why you can't use your kitchen wastebasket as a pail, saving buying and storing a piece of equipment and taking care of a rotten job like keeping the garbage pail clean at the same time. If you think that you're going to be doing a lot of delicate cleaning of upholstery, say, or whole walls, where it's important to rinse with clean water after cleaning with soapy water, and doing this over large areas, then you should probably have two pails. In fact, there are double pails on the market that enable you to put soapy water into one side and clear water into the other. It seems like a fairly good idea, but I don't think it's the sort of thing I would run right out and buy unless I were sure I were going to need it.

A WET MOP

A wet mop cleans dirt off floors that require water and soap to put it into solution. You can clean a floor with a wet rag, if you want to, but, orthopedic surgeons notwithstanding, it's probably easier to move around standing up. Two things to look for in a wet mop (God, what a thought!): First, as with a dry mop, make sure the bottom is detachable from the handle, so you can throw it in the washing machine. Second, get one made of synthetic fiber if you can; it won't get to smelling so bad so fast. And don't buy the most expensive mop. They're expensive because they're heavy and long-lasting. But a lighter, less expensive mop is easier to push around. When your mop is not as absorbent as your cherished memories of it when it and the world were young, it's time to chuck it out and take yourself down to the friendly neighborhood hardware store and treat yourself to a new one. One knows somehow when one's mop isn't as absorbent. Or ask somebody.

Mops should be cleaned when they look rather gray and wretched. Putting them in the washing machine will get the dirt out and adding bleach will make the mop look better—if you care.

By the way, there are several schools of thought on how to mop. There are those who feel that the mop should be barely damp enough to dissolve the dirt. Then there are the sloshers who dip the mop into the pail, lift it out and slog it all over the floor with careless abandon. I am of the rather dryer mop persuasion. Stick the mop in the bucket, wring out the better part of the water with your hands, and mop away.

If your mop starts getting scraggly, trimming the ends will keep it from sloshing against woodwork.

WAX APPLICATORS

Are something you can do without. Basically, they consist of a pad on a stick with a flat, rectangular bottom. The pads that come with the applicator are washable and replaceable and are almost always made of lambswool. You might want a wax applicator if you have lots of floors that you wax frequently: they do keep you upright rather than bending down. It's a good idea to rinse out the pad in soapy water after you use it to apply wax, since it's almost impossible to clean after the wax dries on it. Apply the wax by pouring a little puddle on the floor and spreading it, with the grain of the wood, with the applicator.

FLOOR BUFFERS

Are useful if you have wood floors that you like waxed and shiny. Basically, it's a machine with two pads on the bottom that go around very fast. You can get pads in several materials to fit them: Fine steel wool is good when you're cleaning a waxed floor. Lambswool is excellent for buffing. In either case, try to move the machine along the grain of the wood. Buffers aren't necessary if you have few or no wood floors. Most other floorings will take a self-polishing wax.

AND LAST, BUT FAR FROM LEAST, THE TOILET BOWL BRUSH

The reason you don't use a rag or your whisk broom to clean out the toilet is that there remains in most of us a vestigial dislike of sticking one's hands into a toilet bowl. Overly fastidious, perhaps, but there you are. Brushes, by the way, serve the same purpose as brooms; because of their abrasive qualities, they lift dirt and move it.

Go into the store and ask the nice man for a toilet bowl brush. You can get them in pretty pastel colors to match your bathroom decor and, if you really want to, you can get a container to hold it in the same pretty pastel color. You use the bowl brush in conjunction with a toilet bowl or bathroom cleaning agent (there are lots). On the other hand, you can use bleach if you want to. Read the instructions, which are relatively clear. You may have to do it twice if it's the first time in a long time since you hit the old bowl with a brush. As for cleaning it—not that I spend too much of my time examining other people's toilet bowl brushes —but I've never seen a dirty one. This is probably because it gets itself cleaned and bleached every time it cleans the toilet. So presumably you could use it to scrub vegetables if you ever misplaced your vegetable brush. But you probably wouldn't. Neither would I.

IX

Powders and Potions

OR,
YOU'RE NOT WASHING THE FLOOR WITH SPIC AND SPAN, YOU'RE WASHING IT WITH LOVE AND TRISODIUM PHOSPHATE

The other day, ignoring the peculiar looks shot at me by store managers and fellow shoppers, I counted 213 separate brands of soap, detergent, wax, starch, toilet bowl cleaner, and whatnot on the shelves of the friendly neighborhood A & P. It's sobering to think that man has parlayed a few common garden-variety chemicals and some rudimentary knowledge of what makes women tick into a billion-dollar industry. (It may interest you to know that Proctor and Gamble was the single largest spender of money for advertising in 1969.)

Virtually every soap and detergent and scouring powder, wax remover, wall cleaner, floor cleaner, spray cleaner, and Mother Maybell's Marvelous Mange Remover is made up mostly of one or both of two cheap chemicals, in addition to the soap that the ancient Greeks and Romans used. They are a chemical compound mimicking soap, sodium carbonate (sal soda or washing soda, or soda ash) and trisodium phosphate. Oh, the people at the soap companies may toss in a little bleach, or some ammonia here and there, but that's most of the story. Once you catch onto the make-up of most cleaning products on the market, you should figure out that you can throw out half of what's under your sink.

(Another awfully good reason to throw out half, if not all, of what's under your sink is that trisodium phosphate is what's killing the fish and making the rivers, lakes, and oceans change so alarmingly. Phosphates in running water provide a medium for algae to flourish. These algae are now growing so vigorously they're choking out the fish. The move some time ago to make detergents biodegradable stopped the rivers from filling up with soap bubbles, but detergents, even biodegradable ones, still break down into phosphates, thus causing the above.)

If you would like to run an ecologically pure home, then you should use only Ivory soap (actually any pure soap bar is okay), Ivory Snow, or a detergent containing little or no phosphates, to clean with. In laundering, you may add washing soda as well, if you like flourishes.

What the soap peddlers are peddling, then, is not merely chemical breakthrough, nor is it simply an awareness of most people's desire to get through nasty jobs more quickly. The reason you may have a closetful of redundancies is that these men know what makes most women buy.

They prey on your ignorance. Most women don't know the best way to do things or what gets things clean in the first place. By telling you that this way or that way is the best way, they have a pretty good chance of getting you to listen, since you're not sure of the answer. When the advertising tells you that there is a better way, presumably now the only way, they're appealing to your desire to have some order brought out of the chaos of your life. At least if you know for sure that Glorious Grout Gleamer is the true and only way to get your grout spotless, that's one less thing you have to worry about. Or is it? Who gives a damn about having spotless grout anyway? You do, because:

They play on your guilt. Many women have severe doubts about how well they're fulfilling their role as women, let alone how well they're fulfilling their role as housekeepers, on which they are so frequently judged and on which they so frequently judge themselves. The implication of the advertising is that you will be a better housekeeper and ergo a better woman if you use their product to do a better job, even if the job, when tested in reality, is irrelevant.

They prey on your materialism and on your identification with the objects you possess. If owning a mink coat makes you feel you're a little bit better than your friend with the Persian lamb, doesn't it stand to reason you'll feel a little better than your friend who's still using Brand X, if you've got hold of the new, improved, better variety?

They prey on your predilection, to one degree or another, to take your identity from your possessions. And to identify Glorious Grout Gleamer with the wonderful lady who talks all about it in the television commercials. Maybe, if you have it, you'll have what she has—a happy husband, a hairy dog, love, happiness. Not only because she's standing there showing what she has, but because there's a very real equation in your mind between being a good housekeeper (wife) and winning love and happiness

So now that you understand that it's not Spic and Span that you're washing the floor with, but love and trisodium phosphate, we shall proceed to show you what's really necessary.

We've discussed the basic physical means of cleaning in the last chapter. It's not too difficult to understand the bases for chemical cleaning. Forget about emulsification. Let's stick to a word familiar from television commercials. Soaps, detergents, and household cleaners dissolve the dirt. Alone, or in combination with water, they then float it off the surface from which you're removing it. The stronger the chemical, the more likely it is to dissolve the dirt. However, the stronger the chemical, the more likely it is to damage in some way the material from which it's being removed. That's why you need a variety of things to clean with. Spic and Span, say, used half and half with water, will take the dirt off virtually anything in your house. It will also take the paint off the walls, burn up the fibers in your couch, and take the finish off your dining room table at the same time. So in cleaning, you have to find out what is strong enough to remove the dirt, yet gentle enough not to destroy what you're cleaning. ("The operation was successful but the patient died" seems to be a phrase that applies here. You're operating to remove the dirt; you don't want to kill the surface.)

SOAPS AND DETERGENTS

Detergents are just like soap except that soap has an organic (meaning natural, or not man-made) base and detergents have a chemical or man-made base. "Unbuilt" soaps and detergents are the mildest cleaning agents since they contain no additional chemicals to increase sudsing, help soften hard water, or otherwise improve the cleaning action of the soap (or detergent) in any way. "Built" soaps or detergents contain any or all of the above, but are based primarily on soap and are used primarily for laundering, rather than for household cleaning. We might get to learn more about this if I decide to do a chapter on how to do laundry, but at this point I'm not certain. Why don't you look in the table of contents and if it's there, you can flip to it and find out more if you want to.

At any rate, you use mild soap or detergent for

operating on the most delicate jobs, or when there's not all that much dirt to get off. Ivory Flakes is an example of mild soap. Ivory Liquid, Lux, Joy, and Dreft are all mild detergents.

GENERAL HOUSEHOLD CLEANERS

Come in three forms: powdered, liquid, and spray. All brands are composed primarily of sodium carbonate and TSP; the differences lie only in their concentration, and in their form. Top Job, Janitor in a Drum, Mr. Clean, Spic and Span, Ajax (the kind that comes in a box) are as alike essentially as peas in a pod. You can experiment and find out whether you prefer the powdered or the liquid form of household cleaner, and it's distinctly possible that you may find one that you treasure above all others. Just keep in mind that you don't need more than one. Don't put too much credence in claims that one is all that much stronger than the other. If you need something stronger, just add less water than it says to on the box. If you haven't tried a spray cleaner, like Fantastic, you might pick up a bottle. Although spray cleaners contain the same ingredients as other general cleaners, they can be applied directly to walls, woodwork, or whatever you have dirty, by spraying them on, and require no mixing, pail, or water. So they're handy for quick jobs and for some reason they do seem to work remarkably well. Fingerprints disappear, crud you never knew you had comes off bathtubs (I have a nagging suspicion that there's an additive in them that make your rag look dirtier than dirt), and I think I'll recommend them as an adjunct, if not an absolute necessity.

Abrasive cleansers contain the same ingredients plus a little rough material to add rubbing power to the soap action. The rough stuff is usually feldspar and it works on the same principle as steel wool or sandpaper, only more gently. Cleansers like Ajax or Comet also contain

bleach. Incidentally, before Proctor and Gamble fan-
fared Comet onto the market some ten years ago, they
took a survey to find out what housewives wanted most
from a sink cleaner. And what they found out, strangely
enough, was that they wanted something that would
get their sinks white. (You might take a moment to consider that white does not necessarily mean clean—or
vice versa. Those old rhubarb stains left in the 20-year-
old sink have no germs, bacteria, or lurking sudden
death. They've just dyed the sink a paler shade of
pink.) These marketing research men discovered that
some of these ladies had long been leaving cloths
soaked with bleach in the bottom of their sinks overnight to get the sink pristine. So, Proctor and Gamble
added bleach to their cleaner, stressed whiteness in their
advertising, and Comet went on to become the king
of cleansers with three billion cans sold. It makes one
think. Cleansers seem to me much of a muchness—
you can pick them for their decorator shades or whatever is cheapest. Don't pull all the adhesive off the holes
on top—leave a bit on and less will come pouring out.

Metal polishes ordinarily contain an abrasive, fine
enough not to scratch the highly polished surface but
hard enough to remove the tarnish. These abrasives
are usually suspended in a liquid or in a paste which
also helps remove soil. Liquid polishes are generally
more efficient at removing tarnish. Soap and ammonia
are usually thrown in.

Dishwasher detergent is yet another variation on the
theme of trisodium phosphate, with borax and powdered
soap added.

Ammonia is a gas, sold suspended in water. If you
want to save a little money you can get a stronger solution of ammonia at the drugstore and dilute it yourself. Ammonia makes things like glass and nontarnish-
ing metals shiny, so that's why it's the major ingredient
of Windex.

Soap Pads are made out of steel wool, impregnated

with soap. Steel wool is a strong abrasive and that's why you use it when simply dissolving the dirt won't do and you have to rub it off. You can, if you want to, buy your steel wool in batches at the hardware store and rub it on soap.

If you do buy soap pads like Brillo (isn't that an abrasive name?) do tear them in half and, curiously enough, they'll last twice as long.

Then there are the *waxes and polishes* for floors and furniture, for which see the section on floors and furniture.

Oven Cleaner, Toilet Bowl Cleaner, and *Drain Cleaner* are all predominantly lye. Lye is corrosive, which means it eats away at things. That's why you flush the toilet, pour lots of cold water down the sink, and make sure to clean out the stove, so that the lye doesn't keep eating away enough to eat away at what you were trying to clean.

The chart on pages 167–168 should tell you exactly what ingredients to stock in your cleaning closet. One of each kind should do you. More is redundant and wasteful. If you feel that that chart tells more than you need to know, I'll sum up. What you definitely need:

   mild soap or detergent,
   general household cleaner,
   abrasive cleaner.

All the rest are basically optional and are yours to use if you feel you need them or that they'll make life easier for you. From time to time I may mention other things that are handy, but don't rush right out and get them unless you're contemplating the specific job they're for.

WHAT IT IS	WHAT IT'S FOR	FORMS	BRAND NAMES
Mild detergent	Dishes, cleaning upholstery, other delicate cleaning jobs as noted	liquid granular	Ivory, Lux, Joy (use liquid, it's better)
Mild soap	interchangeable with above except for ecological reasons	bar granular granular	Ivory, Camay Ivory Snow All, Salvo, etc.
Built soaps and detergent	for laundering clothes	granular	Spic and Span Top Job, Janitor in a Drum
General household cleaner	all washable surfaces, cleaning abilities differ in concentration or strength of solution	liquid spray (needs no diluting)	Fantastic, Dow
Dishwasher detergent	washing dishes in dishwasher	granular	All, Cascade
Toilet bowl cleaner	cleaning toilet bowls	granular	Vanish
Drain cleaner	keeping drains clear	granular	Drāno

Item	Use	Form	Brand
Oven cleaner	cleaning ovens	spray	Easy Off, Dow Easy Off (cheaper)
Ammonia	cleaning glass	liquid liquid	straight or in Windex
Steel wool pads	rubbing dirt off, where simple chemical means not sufficient	pads	Brillo, plain
Abrasive cleaner (scouring powder)	adds abrasive rubbing action for cleaning surfaces where chemical means not sufficient	powder	Ajax, Comet
Metal polishes	cleaning and polishing metals	liquid, paste	depends on metal see chapter on
Floor waxes and polishes	waxing and polishing floors and furniture	liquid, paste	floors and furniture
Wallpaper cleaner	cleaning dirt off unwashable wall paper	paste	any brand, varies with locality
Baking soda, cream of tartar, vinegar, salt	miscellaneous jobs—see chapter on how to clean		bought generically, not as brands

A Note About Water

Water turns out to be a generally necessary adjunct to cleaning as you may have noticed. By and large, hot water soups up the cleaning action and makes whatever you're using work better. Do, however, remember that water itself can cause a change in surfaces —wood, fabrics, in fact anything that's porous. So, unless you're dealing with something that has no pores (glass, linoleum, etc.), use it sparingly, as though it were a rare and precious cleaning agent, which after all it may become one day.

How to Set Up Your Equipment

If you have a broom closet, you should be able to get into it:

broom
dust mop
feather duster
wet mop
dustpan and brush
whisk broom
wax applicator.

Hang them on hooks so that their bottoms do not touch the floor. On the shelves on top of the closet store your cleaning materials. Store rags in a bag—a plastic laundry bag would be fine. If you have quite a large house you might think about keeping two cleaning areas. Probably you'll just think about it.

If you're in the habit of buying more than one of a cleaner at a time, put duplicates in rows or one on top of the other. If you insist on buying and holding onto items like Mother Maybell's Grout Cleaner, keep it in a totally different part of the ball park.

If you like to stock up on large boxes, in the belief that you're saving money (which you are, but not all that much—check it out sometime) and you find the boxes too bulky to fit, decant the contents into a container. Square gin bottles take relatively little space. Or try laying the box on its side. If it still won't fit, make a strong mental note that if you hadn't taken so long to fit the bloody box in, you wouldn't have been late getting off to the dentist and you could have walked instead of taking a bus, thereby blowing the thirty cents you saved buying the big inconvenient box.

Keep your repair items like glue, plastic wood, string, and Scotch tape separate from your cleaning stuff, since once mixed together they're almost impossible to extricate from the morass.

In storing your vacuum cleaner, see if you can't hang the attachment bag on a hook. If you've lost the attachment bag invest a dollar in a shoe bag and stuff the attachments in there.

Put together a cleaning box. If you can get hold of a tomato box carrier with a handle from your friendly neighborhood grocer, you're in luck, because it's the perfect size. Stock it with

whisk broom
spray cleaner
dust cloths
a sponge
Ajax or Comet
Windex
an art gum eraser.

Then, as you get ready to clean out the stables or your bedroom, you'll be halfway ready.

And stick in a pair of rubber gloves. Most women have the motherwit to wear rubber gloves for cleaning ovens, where the major component of oven cleaner is lye. Few women, however, bother to wear rubber gloves when washing dishes, wringing out mops, or scouring bathtubs. Well, they're your hands, and maybe Madge the Manicurist knows something I don't, but I find it hard to believe keeping your hands in what is, after all, paint remover, can do them any good at all.

X

After All This Time, How to Clean

THE ELIZABETH TAYLOR WHO'S AFRAID OF VIRGINIA WOOLF TEN-MINUTE CLEAN-UP, THE MILDRED DUNNOCK VERY GROWN-UP AND THOROUGH AND RESPONSIBLE WEEKLY, MONTHLY, AND SEASONAL CLEANUP, AND OTHER THINGS YOU SHOULD KNOW ABOUT HOW TO CLEAN

And so, armed with your cleaning box and the knowledge that your strength is as the strength of ten because your house is totally reorganized, your clutter is deposited out of sight for the moment, your schedule shows that you need work only 2½ hours today, and you were able to face making breakfast with something less than your usual agony because on this morning you at least know what has to be done. Are you happy? Probably not. Because even as a steak and lobster diet begins to pall after a week of nothing else, no system in the world is ever going to make most of us actually enjoy doing housework. (Do remember that at no point did I ever say that I could make you *like* doing it. Or, as I am fond of saying to my son, "You don't have to like it, you just have to do it." I just said I could make you *do* it.)

As we pointed out in the chapter on making a schedule, only you can decide the degree of cleanth that is necessary to maintaining your sanity. And everybody reading this is going to have different ideas on what's necessary to a clean house. All I can do here is to present the most efficient order of cleaning things in any given room. Obviously, there are some jobs I'll include that are inapplicable in your case—you might not have a bedroom for all I know. Or, it may be totally unnecessary to your peace of mind to have dusted picture frames. Nevertheless, I think that just simply knowing what comes when should be another help in ordering your housekeeping and ordering your head.

Keep in mind, by the way, that this is an organizational chapter, and don't panic when you see something like "clean the walls in your bathroom" and you haven't the faintest idea of how to go about it. That's coming in the next chapter, and you'll probably have to do some flipping back and forth at first but I thought about it a whole lot and it seemed better to me this way. For the purposes of this chapter, then, there are only a few things you need to know and a few ground rules you have to follow in carrying out whatever parts of the daily cleaning routines you feel like.

1. It's up to you whether you use a rag, a sponge, a hank of hair, or your husband's clean undershirt when you're cleaning off something that requires the application of some sort of solution. Just make sure you wring it out, so it isn't dripping.

2. A dusting rag means a lintless cloth, cheesecloth, chamois, or whatever you decide to use after reading about rags. Dust wood in the direction of the grain.

3. Household cleaner means medium strength, or it may be described as strong or mild, meaning you follow the directions on the back of the box.

4. Mild detergent solutions mean four squirts of Ivory Liquid or any other mild detergent (or Ivory Snow) in a quart of warm water.

5. Warm water means more hot than tepid, although if you promise to wear rubber gloves you may make it quite hot, unless otherwise noted, and it will clean a bit better.

The Elizabeth Taylor Who's-Afraid-of-Virginia-Woolf Emergency Cleanup

The idea with this one is to do these in order, proceeding from step 1 to step 2 and so forth, if there's time.

What You Need

a carton
a wet sponge with scouring
     powder on it
or damp rag
a carpet sweeper
     (preferably toy)

How Long It Will Take

Whatever you've got

1. Close the doors to any room you know won't be in use.

2. Go through the house with the carton, piling all out of place material into it.

3. Put the dishes into the sink.

4. Make the beds.

5. Wipe any very visible dirt off tables and floors and such with the sponge or rag. Get the bathroom next.

6. Carpet sweep rugs or carpets where there are piles of dirt.

7. Sweep any floors.

The Keep Up a Good Front and What They Don't Know Won't Hurt Them Cleanup

Which should be done any day you want to get the house looking clean. I would say every day, but one must allow for those days when one simply cannot.

Equipment You Need
feather duster
rags (2 damp cleaning kind, 2 dry polishing kind, or paper towels)
whisk broom
toy carpet sweeper
dust mop
sponge
scouring powder
spray cleaner

Time It Will Take
10 minutes to 45 minutes depending how big your place is and also depending on where you stop

The purpose of the general cleaning is not to clean. It is to make things look to the untutored eye as though they are in reality very clean.

CLEANING BASKET

Put the above equipment into your cleaning basket. Actually, it should be in your cleaning basket already, but if it's not for some reason, put it in, with exception of the top carpet sweeper and the dust mop.

BATHROOMS AND BEDROOMS

A. Take the largest wastebasket in the apartment or on the floor. Go from room to room emptying ashtrays and wastebaskets and any other perceivable garbage into it. Wipe out ashtrays with damp rag.

B. Open the windows in the bedroom and throw back the covers of the bed.

C. Open the bathroom window.

D. Go to the kitchen, taking the wastebasket with you. Put the dishes in the sink and return to the bathroom, carrying with you the mop and the carpet sweeper.

E. Put away the toothpaste, etc. Put any miscellaneous clutter in the clutter place.

F. Wet the sponge with scouring powder. Go over the sink, toilet, bathtub, and floor, only where you see dirt. Rinse.

G. If the mirror is noticeably dirty, Windex it. Feather dust the windowsills.

H. Straighten and check the towels, close the shower curtain. Carpet sweep the carpet if there is one, if necessary.

I. Close the window.

Go to the Bedroom

A. Put clutter out of the way.

B. Make the beds.

C. If there is any gross dirt on walls or woodwork remove it with dry rag and spray cleaner.

D. Feather dust tops of tables and dressers, making well-intentioned swipes at things on dressers, telephone, shelves, windowsills.

E. Fluff up pillows on chairs, whisking off, if necessary.

F. Dust mop and/or carpet sweep, as necessary.

G. Open or close curtains according to time of day.

H. Close the windows. (If it's summertime, you might want to leave them all open until you get finished. In dead of winter you might have them open for only a couple of minutes. Work it out for yourself, but do try to have them open a little—it really makes a difference.)

LIVING ROOM, FAMILY ROOM, DINING ROOM, HALL

A. Open windows.

B. Take largest wastepaper basket in area and empty any other wastebaskets, ashtrays, and visible garbage into it. Wipe out ashtrays with damp rag.

C. Put debris in Debris Depot.

D. Feather dust surfaces, as in bedroom.

E. Remove any obvious dirt with spray cleaner and rag.

F. Brush off upholstery if necessary. Fluff up pillows.

G. Carpet sweep and/or dust mop as necessary.

KITCHEN

A. Open window.

B. Put debris in clutter place or drawer.

C. Feather dust windowsills.

D. Wipe up counters, where used, with sponge and scouring powder.

E. Wipe up floors, if there's visible dirt, with sponge, and wipe up visible dirt on stove, refrigerator, et cetera, while you're at it.

F. Empty wastebaskets.

G. Put away cleaning equipment.

H. Close window.

As you can see, the idea is to attack only the visible dirt, and, by feather dusting and wiping up where absolutely necessary, to prevent an accumulation of dirt from rising up to greet you when you come in for your weekly cleaning.

The Mildred Dunnock Very Grown-up and Thorough and Responsible Weekly Cleaning

THE BATHROOM

What You Need

a vacuum cleaner if you have a carpet down, or
a mop or a sponge and a pail if you don't
1 wet rag and 2 polishing rags (or paper towels)
scouring powder and a sponge or
spray cleaner and paper towels or
household cleaner in a pail
window spray
a toilet bowl brush
Vanish
Drāno

Time It Will Take

about half an hour

1. Open windows.
2. Put displaced stuff in displacement center.
3. Put Drāno down the sink.
4. Using brush and Vanish, clean out the toilet bowl.
5. Using sponge and sink cleansing powder, or, if you prefer, spray cleaner and rags—or detergent solution and sponge or rag—wipe sink, bathtub, toilet, including bottoms of fixtures.
6. With dusting rag, dust off window panes. Shake

out curtains. Wipe off windowsills, as with fixtures.

7. Dust pictures, if any. Dust shelves, cabinets, if any, on outside.

8. Polish mirror, using window spray.

9. Clean sink faucets and other metal by spraying with window spray, then wiping dry with clean rag.

10. If carpet, vacuum. If tile floor, sponge up if small, mop if large.

11. Replace towels with new ones. Replace mat.

12. Close windows.

Monthly Cleaning Jobs

Do one of these jobs below each time you give the bathroom a weekly cleaning. If the jobs are rotated, each should be done about once a month.

1. Clean the tile and walls. About 15 minutes before you're ready to clean the bathroom, fill the tub with hot water and close the door. The steam will loosen the dirt. When you come back in, take a rag or sponge, wrung out in household cleaner solution and wipe off the tile surfaces and walls, as well as the soap dishes, shower heads, light bulbs, and fixtures. Go on to weekly bathroom cleaning.

2. Take up the bathroom carpet, if there is one, and wash and dry it. Wash bathroom windows on inside with window spray.

3. Check the medicine chest and weed out, if necessary. Clean inside of cabinet door. Wipe insides of any other cabinets, and check that contents are in order.

Seasonal Cleaning Jobs

1. Curtains—Take them down, have them cleaned, or wash and rehang them.

2. Hamper—Empty it, wipe it out with a mild detergent solution. Leave it open and let the air dry it out.

3. Shades—Take shades (or venetian blinds) off window. Spread out and clean.

4. Windows—Wash inside and out.

5. Medicine chest—Remove contents, weed out, wipe down shelves with mild detergent solution. Let the air dry it and replace contents.

Bathroom Miscellany

If you keep a bottle of detergent near the tub, a bit in the tub will prevent a ring from forming. It will also produce nice bubbles that anyone might enjoy. Some children, however, are allergic to this and may break out in a rash. If that happens, return to ugly tub rings. (Incidentally, the rule in our house is everyone to his own tub ring—I don't see why one person should have to take care of everybody else's.) Even if you don't use it for bubble bath, keep detergent and sponge near the tub and encourage all bathers to clean their own rings.

If you're planning to lay a bathroom carpet, make sure you wash it before you finally lay and cut it to size. They frequently shrink.

If you are bugged by the mirror steaming up, always run cold water first, then hot. The bathroom won't steam and the mirror won't fog.

If hairspray congeals on the mirror, it will come right off with rubbing alcohol.

If there is a nasty smell caused by someone using the bathroom for one of its primary purposes, lighting a match or two will clear the air.

THE BEDROOM
Weekly Cleaning

Equipment	Time
Vacuum cleaner with rug, floor, and upholstery attachments	about 1 hour
Two dusting rags	
One cleaning rag or sponge or paper towels	

Pail of household cleaner solution
Spray cleaner
Whisk broom
Window spray and paper towels
Feather duster
Fresh linens for bed.

1. Open the windows.
2. Put debris in Debris Depot.
3. Strip the bed.
4. Dust wood furniture and headboard of bed. Dust shelves, books.
5. Use upholstery attachment to vacuum furniture, or use whisk broom. Use whisk broom on lamp shades (feather duster if they're delicate).
6. Shake curtains. Dust windows and venetian blinds with feather duster.
7. With molding brush attachments, go over moldings, if any, and baseboards.
8. Vacuum the mattress, using upholstery attachment.
9. Put linens on bed.
10. With damp rag (or sponge or paper towel) wrung out in cleaning solution wipe off windowsills, fingerprints or smudges off walls and woodwork. With damp rag (new one) wipe off anything on surfaces, picture frames, telephones, lamps.
11. If it's a wood floor, first vacuum the rugs, then vacuum the wood floor with the floor attachment.

If it's a carpet, vacuum it.

Monthly Jobs

Do two a week—about a half-hour per job.

1. Brush curtains with whisk broom or with drapery attachment of vacuum.
2. With wall cleaning attachment, dust moldings near ceilings. Or use a dust mop with a rag over it.
3. Straighten out the night tables.
4. Tidy the drawers of one dresser.

5. Tidy up one closet.

6. Turn the mattress (turn it end to end one month, and turn it over the next).

7. Wash the insides of the windows.

Seasonal Jobs

1. Take up the rug and have it cleaned or have the carpet cleaned professionally or do it yourself and clean and wax the floors.

2. Clean and wax the furniture.

3. Take down the curtains, clean and rehang them.

4. Air feather pillows by hanging them outdoors or tumbling them in the dryer with no heat. Don't air foam rubber pillows in the sun, they deteriorate. If you think they're very much in need of cleaning, send them to the cleaner.

5. Clean the closet(s).

6. Wash the windows inside and out.

How to Make a Bed

If you don't know how to make a bed, get someone to show you. You might not know, however, that if a pillow is too large to slip easily into a pillowcase, you do it this way: turn the case inside out. Put your hands in and grab the corners of the case and the corners of the pillow at the same time. Give it a flip around, and voila!

THE KITCHEN

Weekly Cleaning

Equipment	Time
broom	½ to 1½ hours
mop	
pail	
mild detergent	

household cleaner
scouring powder
sponge
floor wax
feather duster
rags—cleaning and soft, or
paper towels

1. Open windows.

2. Examine stove. If burners are too dirty to clean in place with steel wool, soak in sink with strong cleaning solution.

3. Put away all dishes, etc., from dishwasher or drain.

4. Put debris in Debris Depot.

5. Shake out curtains. Dust windows, shades, or blinds.

6. Clean trap in dishwasher.

7. Sweep up floor with broom.

8. Discard all spoiled food from refrigerator and organize what's left.

9. Dust pictures and pantry shelves with damp cloth.

10. Wring out a cloth in mild detergent and wipe around inside of refrigerator.

11. Fill pail with detergent solution and water at moderate strength. With cloth wrung out, wipe the following surfaces:

   a. the outside of the refrigerator
   b. the washer and dryer
   c. the outside of the dishwasher
   d. the windowsill
   e. the outsides of cabinets and the inside parts that you touch frequently with your hands
   f. any other metal, porcelain, or wood surfaces except for the stove and the sink

12. Wipe counters with scouring powder and sponge. Dry with dry rag or paper towel.

13. Wipe stove with scouring powder and sponge. Use steel wool pads where necessary.

14. Put burners back on stove

15. Clean out sink
16. Put Drāno down drain.
17. Empty wastebasket and wipe out inside. Put in new bag.
18. Replace dishtowels and potholders, if necessary.
19. If floor has been waxed recently, damp mop with cold clear water. If in need of rewaxing, scrub floor thoroughly with strong cleaning solution or wax remover and hot water. Rinse with clean water and allow to dry. When dry, apply self-polishing wax with cloth or applicator.

Monthly Jobs
(Do one or two a week—½ hour)
1. Defrost refrigerator
2. Clean stove (oven and broiler)
3. Clean out, with detergent and water, one cabinet or drawer and make certain contents are organized. (This avoids doing them all at once.)
4. Polish the silver
5. Wash windows on inside

LIVING ROOM

Weekly Cleaning

Equipment	Time
vacuum cleaner with rug, floor, wall, and upholstery attachments	¾—1 hour
cheesecloth or polishing rags	
diapers or dusting cloths	
rags or sponge or paper towel	
pail of water and household cleaner	
mild detergent solution	
spray cleaner	
whisk broom	

window spray and paper towel
feather duster

1. Open the windows. However, if you're going to clean the fireplace, keep them closed until after you've finished that.

2. If there's been a fire, brush up the ashes around the hearth with a slightly dampened dustpan and brush.

3. Empty ashtrays, papers, etc., into wastebasket and remove.

4. Put debris in Debris Depot.

5. Dust bookshelves, record shelves, mantel, doors, moldings, and baseboards. Use either the wall attachment brush of the vacuum or a clean cloth, or a very clean dust mop.

6. Vacuum upholstery or brush with whisk broom. Shake out draperies.

7. Dust wood furniture with cheesecloth or polishing cloth. Rub hard to remove fingerprints. If there are encrustations, follow instructions under wood furniture.

8. With a damp soft cloth, wrung out in mild detergent, wipe off decorations on tables, including lamps. Whisk broom shades.

9. Windex windows and mirrors. Windex any glass or chrome furniture.

10. If there's any plastic or lacquer furniture, wipe off with damp cloth wrung out in mild detergent. Polish with cheesecloth or soft dry cloth.

11. Wipe fingerprints or smudges off woodwork, walls, and doors with detergent solution or spray cleaner and rag or paper towel.

12. If there's a wood floor, first vacuum the rug, then vacuum the floor with the floor brush attachment. If there is carpet, vacuum the carpet.

13. Put out clean ashtrays, new magazines, fresh flowers, and so on, depending.

Monthly Cleaning

Choose one job a week.

1. Vacuum rug or carpet thoroughly. Allow about fifteen minutes for a 9 by 12 rug.

2. Go through magazines. Store or throw out the noncurrent ones. Straighten drawers, shelves, cabinets.

3. Make repairs to wood furniture, remove spots from rugs and/or upholstery.

4. Clean inside of windows.

Once or Twice a Year

1. Clean and wax furniture.

2. Clean and wax wood floors.

3. Wash walls.

4. Wash or Windex glass on picture frames.

5. Take down draperies and/or curtains and clean.

6. Have rug or carpet cleaned. Turn the rug the other way when it gets back so that it gets sun equally year by year.

7. Scour the fireplace with steel wool dipped in household cleaning solution.

8. Polish andirons, doorknobs, fireplace tools.

9. Remove books from shelves, wipe shelves out with sponge or rag wrung out in mild detergent solution or stronger solution if they're quite dirty. Dust the books off with a rag before you put them back. By the way, books imported from England frequently warp because of the difference in humidity. So it's a good idea to jam imported books in very tightly.

10. Clean leather furniture.

11. Clean the closets and cabinets.

12. Take down the shades or venetian blinds and clean them.

13. Wash the windows, inside and out.

CHILDREN'S ROOMS

Children's rooms should have the same weekly cleaning as other bedrooms. However, at least once a month, you should make an attempt to sort through toys. Put those infrequently used in a box in the closet and bring them down the following month. While you're doing that, wipe off the toys that look dirty, and keep up with toy repairs. Along with the kitchen, the kids' rooms are most in need of debris collection. You can spend half your time taking toys from here to there and watching them float back again. Since there's a whole chapter on children in the book, I refer you to that for sympathy, succor, and perhaps some helpful advice.

FAMILY ROOM, DINING ROOM, HALL

Clean as living room.

BABY'S ROOM

If you're frantic about having your youngest breathe in only the purest atmosphere, that's up to you. I suggest that you give it a daily once over, a weekly cleaning equivalent to that of any of the other rooms and, about once a month, take in a pail of cleaning solution and wipe down the crib mattress, dressing table, and other surfaces. You could spray with a disinfectant.

Very dirty stuffed animals will sometimes revive if sprayed with a dry cleaner like Goddard's. Cornstarch will work if they're only lightly soiled. Brush it out with a whisk broom.

Seasonal Cleaning

While I've listed such little goodies as taking down the venetian blinds and washing them or cleaning and waxing the floor, in the room by room rundown, you should be aware that there's another way to handle it that might prove more satisfactory to you. This involves doing seasonal cleaning—not room by room, but rather job by job. For instance, floors might be cleaned and waxed on the same day in both the living room, bedroom, and hall. Or all rugs might be taken up and sent out to be cleaned. This is a particularly advantageous system if you can afford to hire a professional cleaning service, since their work is most efficiently done in kinds of work, rather than rooms.

Tasks that can be seasonal:

1. Clean and wax wood floors.
2. Strip kitchen and other tile and linoleum floors completely of old wax and rewax.
3. Clean upholstery.
4. Clean slipcovers.
5. Clean rugs.
6. Wash windows inside and out (the frequency would vary according to the quality of the air in your neighborhood). Where I live, they could do with it weekly.
7. Wash walls.
8. Take down all shades and venetian blinds and clean.
9. Clean and rewax furniture.
10. Clean closets and cabinets.

I don't think it's a particularly workable idea unless you have help, or a small apartment, say a living room, bedroom, and kitchen. Somehow, the sight of that list—to think that you might actually have to do all that in the course of a single little year—is mind blowing, and I, at least, would turn tail and run.

XI

Floors and Walls and Windows and Some Other Things That You May Not Know How to Do All That Well

Now if you've gotten this far, think how far you've come. We began with the premise that there were psychological factors preventing you from simply *doing* things. And we showed you how you could maybe con yourself out of your hangups, leaving you better equipped to tackle the nitty gritty. Realizing, however, that no one has thus far been analyzed long distance through the pages of a book, we pointed out several ways in which you could combat your nuttiness by reality testing. Not satisfied to stop there, we showed you how, if you were willing, you could step by step artificially rearrange your cleaning habits by organizing your time and organizing your home, along the way pointing out one simple housekeeping change that could make life a whole lot easier—creative displacement. (Not trusting any reader to know exactly what was needed to clean or what you did with a tampico fiber broom when you finally got one, we introduced

188

you to the intricacies of the tools of your trade.) In the last chapter we made it possible for the most disorganized among you to find out exactly what you had to do and when you had to do it to clean your house. And now, for those of you who, when told to wax a floor, are not 100 percent sure of whether the same stuff you use in the kitchen can be used on the parquet in the front hall, we present a very specific rundown on actually how to clean things.

It is an awful temptation, once you've found out all the things you always felt guilty about not knowing, to impart the fruits of your research to everyone, with the keen expectation that they've been dying to find out about them all their lives, too. For instance, it was only a month or so ago that I found out how to use bleach. (I'd always had the feeling that it was a dangerous drug, to be used only by dedicated housewives whose mothers had spent the whole of childhood initiating their daughters into the rites and mysteries of housewifeliness.) Actually, it's very easy to use bleach and after I started using it my clothes did look whiter. However, it was hard to stop there and before I knew it I was spending an extra half an hour a week sorting my laundry the right way and probably insuring that my towels would fade a good six months later, but taking time away from things that were somewhat more necessary. It does not happen to matter to me, or to my family, that our clothes are not whiter than white. (Whatever that means. Either they're white or they're dingy gray or yellow or something.) So, with a great scattering to the winds of 3 by 5 cards containing such arcane and helpful information as how to make an adorable centerpiece out of old bottle caps, I have pared this section to the bone and included only those things your average run-of-the-car-pool housewife needs for the maintenance of a well-run house. The test for inclusion was threefold:

1. Would it make a necessary job easier?

2. Would it make a necessary job faster?

3. Would it significantly contribute to future ease or efficiency?

Although what's necessary to me may not by any means be necessary to you and, while I've never washed my walls and have no intention of ever doing so, some of you might feel you have to and for that reason I've told how to go about it if you feel you must. In some cases, where there are two equally good, fast, and easy ways, but one is significantly cheaper, I've included it.

Inevitably a few things have slipped in that are probably neither necessary nor time-saving, but I've tried to keep them to an absolute minimum, taking into consideration that some rather more specific problems might bother some specific people specifically. If you read them and feel guilty that you're not doing them despite everything we've said, forgive me. Try to ignore me and push ever on.

Floors

It is astounding how few people can say with any certainty what's going on underfoot—or what the devil is that stuff they're walking on. You may move into a house or an apartment and be confronted with a veritable bevy of floorings: waxed parquet floor in the living room; linoleum in the kitchen; carpet in the bedroom, and tile in the bathroom. But you're going to have to know more than that if you expect to have any success caring for them. Probably some minimal knowledge exists in the most hopeless household idiot—you don't wax the carpet or shampoo the linoleum—but there's a lot more to it.

Wood Floors

Most wood floors you're likely to encounter will have, or should have, wax on the top, and a finish over the wood itself. With one exception, which we will get to later, unless a stain or spot gets past the wax into the finish, you need concern yourself only with the wax surface. Wax protects the surface, repels water, and keeps things from getting to the finish which is harder than wax to repair, or, heaven forbid, to the wood itself.

Wood floors should be waxed once or twice a year, preferably with a paste wax, buffed, say, once a month with an electric buffer and cleaned about once a week with a dust mop. When you use a dust mop, it's best to move it, if you can, with the grain of the wood.

HOW TO WAX A FLOOR:

1. Remove the old wax by going over the floor with steel wool pads on an electric floor waxing machine. If any crud remains, you should be able to get it up with a cloth dipped in a solution of mild soap suds and wrung out well. Dry it with a clean dry cloth. Dry it again. (If water gets into wood it can cause it to warp.)

2. Following the directions on the can of paste wax (Butcher's Wax is best; Johnson's Paste Wax is okay), apply it to the floor. (You can use a liquid wax like Preen or Simonize. They're easier to apply, but don't give as strong a coat. You can't, however, use the kind of water-based self-polishing wax that you use on the kitchen floor, since its water base will raise the grain of the wood. If you have some stuff around, make sure you check out whether or not it's meant to go on wood.)

3. Buff it well with the floor polisher, using lambs-wool pads. The higher the gloss you get when you buff, the less slippery the floor will be. It's a smeary coat of wax that causes spills.

4. When you're waxing your floors, wax the bottoms of chairs and tables—it's not necessary to buff them. This will keep the floor from getting scratched.

Never use oil, polish, or an oil mop on a waxed wood floor—oil streaks the wax. Never allow water to sit on the floor, and never scrub the floor with water. Water removes the wax, gets past the finish down into the wood, raises the grain and the whole thing is a total mess.

The Exception: A floor that is finished with a penetrating oil finish. If you have a floor that falls into this class you really ought to consider putting a coat of wax on top of it, which will improve its resistance to chipping, scratching, stains, and water spotting. (Oil finish floors are the least slippery when waxed.) However, if you don't choose to wax them, they should be dusted regularly with a dust mop; never buff and, two or three times a year, clean and reoil by taking equal parts of boiled linseed oil and mineral spirits, sloshing it on with a mop and rubbing across the grain with a small stiff brush. Remove the excess with a dry mop and do it again the next day. Don't walk on it for at least twenty-four hours.

White spots: If water or some other liquid has gotten onto your floor, chances are it's not gone further than the wax. Try: (1) rubbing the spot with paste wax; (2) rubbing it hard with a piece of wool cloth; (3) rubbing it with 000 or 0000 steel wool and rewaxing with paste wax; (4) rubbing it gently with turpentine and rewaxing. (Oil finish floors rarely spot. If yours does, rub it with 000 or 0000 steel wool and apply a little bit of half boiled linseed oil, half mineral spirits mixture.)

You really ought to have your floor professionally cleaned and waxed every couple of years, if you can. At present in New York City it's about 10¢ a square foot. A 20- by 10-foot room would run you about $20.00.

LINOLEUM AND ALL THAT

The chances are that the floor in at least one room (probably the kitchen) will be a hard-surfaced, relatively non-porous, man-made material. For the same reason that wood gets protection from wax, so does linoleum and its brothers. But the story here is a little tricky. For most hard-surfaced floors (linoleum, asphalt, vinyl, vinyl asbestos, terazzo, rubber) you may use a water-based self-polishing wax, like Glo-Coat, Beacon, or Bravo. Follow the directions on the can, since they vary, but the point is that no buffing is required since they dry shiny.

Once or twice a year, you should strip off the old wax with a wax remover like One-Step or Butcher's Wax Remover. (A solution of ½ cup Spic and Span, 11 ounces of household ammonia, dissolved in one gallon of warm water, will do the same job more cheaply.) You may have to go over the floor more than once. You'll know that the old wax is off when the floor no longer looks yellow or streaky. Apply the new coat of wax evenly; the best way is to pour a bit into a paint roller pan and dip a lambs wool wax applicator into it, spreading it evenly over the floor. You might as well do it twice.

Most water-based floor waxes are resistant to washing with household cleaner and water. So you can mop them up as needed, once a week or so, with a medium strength solution of Spic and Span or Top Job. Or you can use a cleaner-waxer like Armstrong's One-Step Floor Care, although this will cause a greater build-up of wax.

Cork floors should not be waxed with a water-based self-polishing wax. They should be treated like wood, waxed with a liquid oil-based wax like Preen, and buffed. Linoleum, by the way, can take an oil-based wax or a water-based wax, although why anyone would want to bother buffing a floor unnecessarily is beyond me. Waxed cork floors can be damp mopped, but be sure to have the mop well wrung out and use a mild detergent solution.

CARPETS AND RUGS

Two bad things happen to carpets and rugs. First, dust, if it's not removed, gets set in the fibers and discolors and/or deteriorates them. Second, things get spilled on them. The first you can prevent with some effort by getting up surface dirt at least once a week with a vacuum cleaner and going over them thoroughly about once a month (that means six or seven passes over each spot with the vacuum cleaner.)

Spots and stains are a different matter. The thing is to get them up as soon as possible, since moisture rots the fibers. If the spill is just water, blot it up fast (stick a wad of paper towels under a rug.) If it's something else and it's still there after you've blotted it up and let it dry, try a little carbon tetrachloride on a cloth. Or a cloth with clear water. Dry it well. (You can turn an electric fan on a carpet to help it dry faster.) If you know that the stain is a grease stain, a dry cleaner like Glamorene, sprinkled on and then vacuumed up according to the directions on the can, may do the job. If none of these work, perhaps you can live with it till it's time to get it professionally cleaned.

Speaking of which, you really ought to send out your rugs and have someone come in to clean your wall-to-wall carpeting once a year. They'll look better and last longer. However, if you feel that you must do it yourself, there are three methods.

1. Dry cleaning with a powder that is sprinkled on and then, after it's dried, vacuumed off. Glamorene and Powderene are two brands you might use.

2. Wet shampooing, for which a shampooing ma-

chine is needed. (Some electric floor polishers are equipped to dispense shampoo.)

3. Foam spray, where you spray the foam on in a thin layer, sponge it in with a sponge mop, and vacuum it off when it's dry.

If you decide to try any of these, follow the directions on the can scrupulously and don't plan anything else that day. (Also you'd better not plan anything for that evening either, since most home-cleaned carpets can't be walked on for anywhere up to twenty-four hours.)

Things you should know about carpets:

1. Never use soap, ammonia, washing soda, or any other non-special-for-rug cleaning agents on them. They'll rot or discolor the fibers.

2. Turn area rugs once or twice a year to distribute the wear.

3. If you happen to move your furniture and are bothered by the big dents that show where the chair legs used to be, try brushing the carpet back into place with a stiff brush that's been moistened slightly with warm water. (Casters help some, but they still make dents and I think they look ugly.)

4. Don't worry about fluff coming up from a new carpet. It's normal and it may take up to six months to go away altogether.

5. If your rug sprouts, that is, if a tuft rises above the pile, snip it off even with the rest of the carpet. Don't yank it out.

6. If a carpet develops ripples during very damp weather it's a natural effect of the humidity and it should go back to normal when the weather gets dryer. If it doesn't, you can have the carpet restretched.

7. Don't beat your rugs. It weakens the backing.

Other kinds of rugs:

Indoor/outdoor carpets are made of a synthetic material that resists staining. Most spots just blot up but, since the fibers aren't damaged by water, you can scrub out spots as you would on a hard-surfaced floor.

Fiber, sisal, rush, and grass rugs seldom spot and really just need to be swept from time to time. If you have rush or grass rugs and they seem to be drying out, you can hose them down outside.

Walls and Woodwork

I really do hope you can get somebody else to wash your walls, because it's among the less rewarding pastimes extant. I'm not talking about the fingermark removal we discussed in the last chapter, but your basic, no-nonsense wall washing, which should probably be done once a year. On every wall. In every room. Those of us who are lucky enough to live in apartments that get painted free every two or three years (forgetting that the little service is part of the exorbitant rent we pay) are not terribly likely ever to wash a wall. We just spend the last six months wishing it would be painting time. For everyone else, this is how it's done.

1. Get two pails. And get two sponges. Fill one pail with a mild soap like Ivory Snow or a mild detergent like Ivory Liquid. Then add warm water and take your eggbeater (yes, I said take your eggbeater) and make it very sudsy. Fill the other pail with plain clear warm water.

2. While you are doing this you may cogitate on the concept of wall washing. Walls are covered with paint. (They're covered with other things too, but we'll get to that later. We are now talking about your common, garden-variety painted wall.) Now the problem is, as I think I mentioned somewhere before, that

the same things that take dirt off also take paint off. So you must strike a reasonable balance. If your walls are not too dirty, the mild solution described above will remove the dirt that the vacuum cleaner didn't, if you happened to vacuum your walls from time to time. On the other hand, if the only thing you've done to your walls is to remove the more unsightly murals, there is going to be a buildup of dirt that will laugh at Ivory Snow. It is sending a boy to do a man's work (or a girl to do woman's work is probably more to the point). Therefore, if you know your walls are very dirty, and you think you can do with several millimeters less of paint on them, substitute a relatively mild solution of Spic and Span or Top Job or some other household cleaner for the Ivory. Then proceed. If, by the way, you need more proof of this, consider what comes off on your rag when you wipe a spot off the wall with, say, Fantastic. That chalky white stuff along with the dirt happens to be paint. Then proceed as follows:

3. Dip sponge in soap and wring out well. Then apply said sponge to said wall, rubbing with a gentle circular motion. You must work from the bottom up, since dirt streaking down below where you're working is very hard to get off. Really. Do this earthshaking work over a smallish area, say about two feet square. Then take your other sponge, the one without the soap, and rinse off the soap on the wall. You do this because soap left on walls, as on anything else, leaves a film that catches and holds dirt. Wipe it dry with a soft clean cloth. Then go on to your next two-foot-square area.

4. When the water in either pail gets decidedly dingy, change it. It is not wise to put dirt back where it came. Redundant.

That's it for painted walls, folks. It might help you out to know that the shinier the paint, the less likely it is to rub off, since it's made of stronger stuff. But the walls that one washes when one washes walls are generally wall walls, and very very dull.

Woodwork is not so very different. In fact it's not at all different, except that there's less of it and you are therefore far more likely to undertake that project. You do it precisely the same way.

Spots on a painted wall can usually be removed as presumably you have been doing all along with a spray cleaner. Crayon responds to paste wax. And if there are spots that absolutely won't bow out, white shoe polish makes a fairly decent match with white walls.

Now supposing you have other things on your wall besides paint and pictures. You may have:

Wood Paneling or Wood Doors

In which case you treat them as you would wood floors. Which is to say, you wax them with paste wax and, not being able to buff them with a buffer, you use a dry piece of cheesecloth to get up the shine.

Wallpaper

If you have vinyl-backed wallpaper (Sanitas, for example) you may treat it fairly roughly, using a household cleaner and water, either going over the whole thing or just removing spots. If it is not a plasticized paper, it will respond to water the way paper responds to water, which is to say not very well. I do hope you know the sort that you have. If you're in doubt, test a little spot behind a picture. In any case, don't use too much water.

If your wallpaper is not washable, you will have to get hold of some wallpaper cleaner at the hardware store. It has a rather doughy consistency, which is not surprising considering that its main component is gluten (in fact, you can do a pretty good job of getting marks

off wallpaper with a scrunched-up piece of rye bread—
or an art gum eraser).

By the way, if you happen to be in the process of
wallpapering, do choose a washable paper—they're not
all plums and peaches. And write down behind a picture the number of rolls you used, the cost and, if you
think you might ever want to use it again, the manufacturer and the pattern. Then the next time you want
to do it, you're ahead of the game.

If someone (your child, probably) should happen to
get a piece of Scotch tape on the wallpaper and it is
beginning to yellow and it is in a particularly promi-
nent place, it can be removed by holding a warm (re-
peat warm) iron up close to it, which will sizzle it and
make it fall down dead. On the other hand you should
be aware that you are gambling a relatively inoffensive
piece of Scotch tape for a big burn in the middle of
your wall.

Tile Walls

I think we pretty well covered washing these in the
bathroom.

Tile Film: Even after you've washed the walls, film
may remain. If it bothers you, take a piece of steel wool
without soap. The film will come off like talcum powder.
Then go over the tile with a damp rag wrung out in
household cleaner.

Grout: The grout, the crumbly stuff between the
tiles, frequently is discolored and grungy looking. This
may be from old age or it may be from mildew. In any
case, if it doesn't come white and it bothers you after
washing the tile, you can touch it up with a white finger-
nail stick, or white shoe polish on a Q-tip.

Closets

I'm not entirely sure why I put them here, except that they do have walls in them. The organization of closets has been discussed already. Wash the closet walls the same way you wash wall walls (and wash the shelves and things in there at the same time). Only add some pine oil disinfectant to the water and when you get through spray the closet with moth preventive.

Windows and Surrounding Territory

Where we live it's seven stories up and both of us have a kind of a thing about hanging out a window seven stories off the ground. On the other hand, it costs $1.00 to wash a window and I won't bother you with the statistics, but if we had them washed once a month that would be over $150.00 a year. It therefore came as a revelation to discover that you can clean half of the windows and they will be cleaner than if you don't clean them at all. The half that you clean, and that I've suggested in the cleaning plans, is the inside half.

If you're not washing too many windows at once, the best way to do it, whether you're doing both sides or just the inside, is to use window spray or something like that. It will pay if you run your feather duster over the inside before you begin to spray.

There's another solution that you can use, which is cheaper and I think probably easier for a large number of windows.

1. Fill a pail with 4 tablespoons of ammonia and 1 quart of warm water (or 12 tablespoons of ammonia and 3 quarts of warm water—cleaning is something like cooking). Apply this to the window with a rag (lintless) and wipe it off with a squeegee. (If you're using window spray, use paper towels.)

2. I forgot to mention that you should pick a cloudy

day to do this rather than a sunny one (which should add to your depression about washing windows considerably) since the outsides of windows dry less streakily.

3. When you're wiping it off or squeegeeing it off, use horizontal stroke on the inside and vertical strokes on the outside, or vice versa. This enables you to see where you missed.

4. If you want a nice gleam to the windows, you can take some balled-up newspaper and rub it over the windows. Don't ask why it works.

5. If you are insane enough to wash windows outside on a day when it's below freezing, use 4 tablespoons of denatured alcohol instead of the ammonia and wipe with a chamois and it won't frost up.

Windows generally have something over them and we will deal with them next. We will not, however, deal with draperies and curtains, feeling that it is somehow more allied with upholstery. Anyway, there's enough to do without window hangings. However, the chances are you probably have either shades or venetian blinds. Hopefully, you have been keeping the dust off them with weekly cleaning, using the vacuum cleaner— or something.

Venetian Blinds

To get the dust off, vacuum with the attachment, paying some attention to the tapes while you're at it. Or, if you like it better you can use thick gloves, which you run over the slats. Art gum eraser will take care of smudges. If, however, you want to take more drastic action and actually clean them, do this:

1. Get a pail of household cleaner and water and go over the slats with a damp rag, or

2. Immerse them in a detergent solution in the bathtub, or

3. Throw them over the line you hang your laundry

on, and after you've soaped them, rinse them by turn-ing the hose on them.

If your cords and tapes have turned dingy and gray and you want to remedy it, roll up the cords and dip them in a concoction of ¼ cup bleach and ½ cup water for one minute. Then you can do it again. Tapes, if they don't respond to the detergent and water treat-ment, can be whitened with white shoe polish thinned about half and half with water.

Shades

Before you wash them, if you feel you have to wash them, make sure you can wash them by testing a small area. If it dries up without any visible signs of harm, you can go ahead and do this:

1. Take down the shade. Put it on a large table.

2. Make eggbeater type suds of Ivory Snow or Ivory Liquid and water. That's in one pail. In another pail put clean clear warm water (that's right, just like the walls). You also need two sponges, one for each bucket. Wring the sponge out well and rub with a circular motion in a small area at a time, then rinse, then dry with a clean dry cloth, proceeding until you've got the whole shade as clean as it's going to be.

3. Put the shade back up in the window, which hopefully is shady, and don't roll it up until it's dry.

Screens

When you give them your once a year cleaning, if you do, turn the hose on them, scrub them with deter-gent solution and a scrubbing brush, and then hose them down again. Someone suggests that you hose them down periodically when the urge comes over you, but it seems to me that this would direct the dirt onto the window. Someone also says that wiping the screens with kerosene and then wiping it off will keep aluminum from pitting.

What strikes me as a good idea, if you put screens on by the season, is to number them and the window they correspond with, which should save some jigsaw puzzling.

Windowsills

Treat windowsills when you have to wash them exactly like woodwork. With two exceptions:

1. If they're greasy kitchen windowsills, you can dissolve the grease by washing with a solution of washing soda.

2. If they're revolting rain-spotted, rubbing alcohol will remove the rainspots.

Some people feel that windowsills should be waxed. Others feel that they shouldn't because when it comes to a repainting, not all the wax can be removed and it makes the paint job less smooth.

Wood Furniture

Wood furniture, like wood floors, comes in a variety of finishes and the confusion on how to take care of them is pretty widespread. However, if you look around your house you'll probably be able to divide the furniture into roughly two classes: the shiny and the dull. Shiny furniture generally has a finish made of varnish; smooth wood, which appears to have open pores, has an oil finish. Most contemporary furniture—teak, rosewood, often walnut—is oiled.

How to Care for Shiny Furniture:

The best and ultimately easiest way to keep up shiny surfaced wood furniture is to lay down a good coat of paste wax (Butcher's is about the best) once or twice a year. Liquid wax is easier to apply, but it doesn't set up as much of a protective surface, and furniture oils, while they give the wood a shine, don't do anything at all to protect it. Spray polishes (like Pledge or Simonize Tone) are handy if you want to give your furniture a quick shine but they contain silicones that build up on top of the wax and are hard to remove and, if they're not rubbed in very thoroughly, they attract dust and fingerprints.

Ideally, you ought never to use polish, and just dust the wood with cheesecloth, rubbing harder to get fingerprints out. If you do succumb to polishes, make sure to follow the directions on the can and, if you're doing a large surface, do it a little at a time.

How to Wax:

1. Remove the old wax and dirt by making a solution of 3 tablespoons boiled linseed oil, 1 tablespoon turpentine (this gets rid of the silicone buildup) and one quart of warm water. Dip a rag in, wring it out well and go over the surface. Dry it quickly and well with a clean dry cloth. If anything is left, it's probably water soluble and you may remove it with a cloth that's been dipped in a mild soapsuds solution (use Ivory) and wrung out very well. Dry it, and then dry it again.

2. Apply the paste wax according to the directions on the can. But make sure to rub it in very well, until it has a high gloss. A second application is a good idea.

How to Care for Oil-Finish Furniture:

While spray polishes and paste waxes won't kill oil-finish furniture, they tend to give it a shine that isn't quite what's wanted. Oil finishes are relatively water resistant—but not totally, so you really should use coasters. Dust the wood with a lintless cloth. Reoil it once or twice a year with a solution of half boiled linseed oil and half turpentine, rubbing it in well with a piece of 000 or 0000 steel wool (your hardware store has it—don't for God's sake use regular Brillo-type steel wool pads; they're much too rough). If the furniture seems extremely dirty to you, make the solution a little heavier on the turpentine. Let it sit about ten minutes and then wipe off the excess with a clean, dry, lintless cloth.

There's something called Teak Foam, which is essentially the above ingredients in a spray foam form that works quite well. If you spray it on once a month or so, it will keep your furniture looking good.

White Rings, Black Rings, Lord of the Rings, Scratches, Cigarette Burns and People Who Go Bump in the Night and Knock Your Table Over

Fortunately, most of the ghastly things that happen to furniture seldom go beyond the top layer of wax and into the finish or the wood itself.

Scratches, probably the most common insult to furniture, can be dealt with in a number of ways. Try them in this order. The easiest is first:

1. Apply some paste wax to the area and rub it in.
2. Rub the scratch with a cut walnut; if the wood is light, use a cut pecan.
3. Fill in the scratch with a brown crayon of the appropriate shade.
4. If it's a dark wood, fill the scratch in with iodine.
5. Run an eyebrow pencil over it and smear it around. Those are the easy ways, and in this case there's no best way. You have to find the one that works. If the scratch is still there and you're feeling a

little silly with nuts and crayons and iodine on the coffee table, you can either call in a furniture refinisher or convince yourself that it adds character to the piece or, if you're brave, do the following:

1. Clean the area with a cloth moistened with benzene or carbon tetrachloride; sand the scratch with 000 steel wool to smooth the edges; wipe the area clean and apply a thin coat of varnish; let it dry about ten minutes, then varnish it again three or four times until the scratch is filled in; rub the area with 000 steel wool until it's level with the rest of the surface, then wax the entire surface.

Burns and gouges are best left to furniture refinishers, although you may try a variation of the above: Scrape out the area (a pen knife might do the job); sand it with 000 steel wool; wipe it clean; fill in the area with something called "Dectostick," a sort of stick of wax that you can probably pick up at your local lumberyard (follow the directions, which essentially call for you to melt it and drip it in); wax over the area.

White Spots and Rings on Shiny Furniture

These jobbies are usually caused by something quite hot, something quite cold, or something quite wet that's been left sitting on the surface. That's why you use coasters or trivets. Or you should. It's true that they're making some wood furniture nowadays with an alcohol-resistant and water-resistant finish, but unless you buy it new and ask if it is or not, there's no way of knowing without risking a white ring. On the same order is a kind of white haze, that looks as though someone pushed an iron over the table. On white spots and rings, try the following, going on to the next if the preceding step doesn't work:

1. Rub it with mayonnaise
2. Rub it with paste wax

3. Rub a little cigar ash, if you have some around, onto the ring with your moistened finger.

4. Dampen a small cloth with ammonia and whisk it over the surface; don't rub.

5. Go over the entire surface with grade 000 or 0000 steel wool. Then rewax it. Never use sandpaper or pumice or rottenstone.

6. Wet the surface with mineral oil and rerub where there's still haze or a ring. Dry with a clean cloth and rewax with paste wax.

Oil-finish furniture rarely develops rings, but, if yours has, rub the area down with 000 steel wool and reoil it.

Black Spots sometimes appear instead of white spots and are also caused by moisture. If this happens:

1. Get some oxalic acid crystals (try a paint store or a hardware store); dissolve the crystals in hot water— about 3 tablespoons to a cup, until you're pretty sure the solution is saturated (keep adding crystals until you see some undissolved in the bottom of the cup); brush or rub the solution onto the marks. Wipe the surplus a few times with a damp cloth, let it dry, and rewax it.

That about does it for wood, except to mention that crayon marks will usually come off with paste wax; if some paper gets stuck onto your wood, wet it down with boiled linseed oil and let it sit a bit before peeling it up gently. Go over the area with a mild soap and water solution and rewax it.

If any of your drawers are sticking, rub the runners with paste wax, or soap, or candle wax, whatever happens to be nearest at hand.

Upholstery and Curtains

This is a very touchy subject, because I feel that you can go only so far on your own with fabrics and then you need professional help. However.

Upholstery

By which we mean furniture that is covered in fabric. Of course there are all different kinds of fabric and a Louis XV side chair covered in Scalamandré silk gets different attention than a Naugahyde club chair. It's now quite common for fabrics to have a protective finish on them, which helps to a degree.

You should be keeping the dust from settling into the chairs or whatever by vacuuming weekly, making sure you get into cracks and don't skip around the seams.

The problem here is twofold. On the one hand, upholstery does get dingy after a while. I strongly recommend having it professionally cleaned, which is far less expensive than reupholstering if you happen to do a less than perfect job of applying the cleaning solution. However, if you insist, the safest way is to do it this way, testing a small, inconspicuous part first.

1. Make a whipped suds solution of one part mild soap or detergent to four parts warm water. Have another bucket of clear warm water at the ready. Apply the suds solution very lightly and very gingerly to the fabric, rubbing with a gentle circular motion. Rinse it the same delicate way with the other damp sponge. Another way of generally cleaning upholstery is with commercial dry cleaners like Glamorene. I will be perfectly frank and say that I've never done this. So if you want to, just read the directions carefully and pray.

The same problem presents itself with getting spots

off upholstery. If the material is Scotchgarded, the liquid should sit on top of the fabric for a little while before sinking into the fibers. But only for a little while. It doesn't mean that it won't spot. It just means that if you get after it within a reasonable amount of time, you have a good chance of blotting it up. Blot it up with paper towel. If a spot persists, or if there's a spot in a non-Scotchgard material, you can try the suds method, which will remove most food stains. Or you can use the dry cleaning method, depending on which is better suited to your material. Ah, well. I fear that in the area of upholstery I'm not of much help, being somewhat squeamish about the whole thing. Proceed at your own risk.

You can relieve some of the wear and tear on your upholstered pieces if you upend the cushions if you happen to be going away for a while.

Slipcovers

Slipcovers are a rather simpler matter, being (a) removable, and (b) made of generally sturdy materials. You vacuum them, of course, to keep the dust from sinking in. If there's a spot, you try to remove it the same way you remove any spot from fabric (making sure whatever you're using doesn't leak down to the upholstery which you're trying to save by having slipcovers in the first place). Slipcovers can be removed and cleaned when they're very dirty. But it's a good idea to throw them in the dryer every three months or so and tumble them for fifteen minutes with no heat. This will tumble out a good bit of dust.

Draperies and Curtains

Once again, assuming you've been keeping most of the dust off them, you have the choice of either cleaning them yourself or having them professionally cleaned.

Certainly good draperies should be cleaned professionally about once a year. You can take your chances with spot removal, as per instructions in the spot-removal section.

Curtains are generally washable, according to what kind of material they are. If you'll hang your curtains up while they're still damp, you may save yourself some ironing.

While you may not want to tackle cleaning draperies yourself, there's no reason why draperies and curtains can't be tumbled in the dryer the same way slipcovers can. Window coverings do get dirty pretty easily, occupying as they do the place between you and dirt from outside. As with upholstery, cleaning draperies and curtains is not a purely esthetic measure, since dirt allowed to remain in fabric weakens the fibers and produces a shorter life.

You should, once a year, when you take down your draperies to clean them, see if you can't switch panels, since that will even out the wear and, if the left side of the living room gets more sun than the right, you won't wind up with a disparity of several shades between two panels if you do that. Same thing goes for curtains. And don't let your window curtains hang so that their hems are in direct contact with the windowsill. Make them either a bit shorter or longer and they won't pick up as much dirt at the bottom.

How to Clean Things in the Kitchen

How to Defrost a Refrigerator
Given a choice between defrosting a refrigerator and cleaning out an oven, I suppose I would have to choose the refrigerator, although it's rather like being asked whether you'd prefer to take your vacation in Siberia or Hoboken. Really, really, really, it's not so horrible if

you do it every other week, or even once a month, or even every two or three months. It's just that some of us leave it for a year and the freezer is so crammed with ice that the only thing that fits in there is a can of frozen chives.

1. Turn off the refrigerator or turn it to defrost and let it sit for a while, depending on what you happen to be doing. Call a friend and bitch about what an awful morning you're having.

2. You must now remove the food from the freezer. For years I stacked it on counters, where it melted all over, or in the bottom of the refrigerator where it melted all over and then, one morning, in that flash of inspiration that reveals true genius, my eye caught—the dishwasher. So put your food in the dishwasher, or the washing machine, or in a vegetable crisper. By the way, try not to plan a refrigerator defrosting for the day after you bring home a $75.00 market order. You remove food from the freezer in order to clean it. You also remove food from the refrigerator so the ice doesn't drip down on it too much.

3. Put a whole lot of folded newspaper on the top shelf. This will absorb the water and ice that comes cascading out. You could use a turkish towel but it gets all soggy and icy, but *chacun à son goût.*

4. The next job is to get that old ice to melting. There is a little gadget whose name I forget, but it looks like a small electric squash racket and it heats up and you put it in the freezer. Move it around so that it points up at the ice. Should you not have this gadget, nor be willing to part with the money (it makes a good thing to split with a friend—about three dollars each. After all, the probability that you and she will be seized with the desire to defrost on the same day is about as remote as both of you having an overwhelming desire to clean the oven.) Several possibilities are open to you. One that is not is to fill your ice-cube trays with hot water—very hot water takes the coating off that

makes them slide out. (You shouldn't ever wash them in hot water either—although why anyone would want to wash ice-cube trays . . .)

A. Your portable hair dryer turned on hot.

B. Pots of hot water.

Both of the above have their disadvantages since with the one you have to stand there the whole time, and with the other you have to keep changing pots of water, to say nothing of slopping it all over the floor.

By whatever means, the heat should loosen the ice. You are now able to do a few things about the ice there. You can use your hands (and if they get too cold, use your oven mitts, they keep out cold, too), an old back scratcher, a wooden spoon. To tell you the truth, I have been using a dull knife all these years and I never so much as tickled a coil (one gets to know where they are) but I would hate to feel guilty of urging you on to such a ghastly indiscretion.

5. Once you get the ice off, by whatever means, take a rag, put it in a solution of baking soda and water and wipe the freezer out. Use detergent on the plastic door liner, the porcelain, and the gasket.

6. Put the food back in the freezer.

7. If you're going on to clean the refrigerator, too, leave the refrigerator off. Wipe down the inside of the refrigerator with baking soda solution. The outside, porcelain, and rubber get a mild detergent (say Ivory Liquid) wipedown. Don't forget to wipe off the light. Should you be so motivated, you can put some vanilla on a piece of cotton and stick it in back of the refrigerator and it will smell nice. But then, I think refrigerators smell nice all by themselves.

By the way, if it makes you feel more virtuous, it costs more to run a frosted-up refrigerator. The coils have to work harder to get it cold. Conversely, if you live in the backwoods where the electricity goes on and off like a firefly, it pays you to keep your freezer stocked full, since if the current accidentally shuts off, food in a full freezer keeps about forty-eight hours and food in a half-full freezer only about twenty-four hours. This assumes you do not open the door, or anything foolhardy like that.

The Oven (or Range or Stove, depending on your age, location, and socio-economic status)

1. If you have any choice, don't get an oven with a glass door. It's one more thing to clean. If you have to clean it, use a solution of baking soda and water and a rag or a paper towel.

2. If you have any choice and a whole lot of money, get a self-cleaning one, because oven cleaning is probably the single most despicable job around the house—anyway, it ranks up there with swabbing down the chimney and looking through the diaper pail for the wedding ring you dropped.

CLEANING AN OVEN

1. There are two prophylactic measures you can take:
   a) Right this minute line the bottom of the oven and the broiler pan with foil.
   b) Try to wipe up spills as they occur.

2. Start the night before by putting all the removable parts from the stove top and broiler pan in your kitchen sink or you could use the bathtub but I hope they all fit in the kitchen sink, along with ½ cup of dishwasher compound and very hot water. Soak till the next morning.

3. Clean what's left of the top of the stove with a rag and hot, strong detergent solution.

4. Paint oven cleaner on the inside of the oven, the way they say on the tube or jar, or spray can. The spray does seem somewhat more esthetic and less fraught with possibilities of death and dismemberment if you get some in the wrong place. WEAR RUBBER GLOVES. That's *lye* they've got in there.

5. Wash off the soaking parts with steel wool or a stiff brush. Drain the sink and refill it with hot detergent water and rinse them in that.

6. Clean out the inside.

7. Have large martini and plot horrible things to do to your husband.

8. If you have any strength and the smell of that stuff is making you sick, scare up an orange peel and put it into a 350° oven.

The Sink

It's a very curious thing about home ownership. Ever since our apartment entered the throes of going co-op, I have stopped throwing my bacon grease down the drain. Bacon grease (and any grease for that matter) is bad for drains because it goes down hot, gets cold in the pipes, congeals and blocks up things. If you throw grease down, not only will you come to grief eventually, but so will the lakes and rivers into which your sewage drains. Fish are not particularly fond of grease. If you pour your bacon grease into a coffee or juice can you will (a) be saving money because you will use it instead of butter for sautéing things, if they're not too delicate (great for deep-frying French fries); (b) be minimizing the possibility of a stopped-up drain; (c) be living ecologically. It seems a rather valuable idea.

Sinks are almost always either porcelain or stainless steel. To clean porcelain, sprinkle cleanser (preferably one with bleach, like Comet) over and around the sink and scrub it with a nylon-mesh ball or a sponge. If stains are too ghastly to bear, you could try putting a wad of paper towels in the sink some night, saturating it with bleach and you can wake up all rosy and expectant about how all those ugly food stains will be banished.

Stainless steel sinks stand up nicely if you rub them with some olive oil on a cotton ball once a week. To eliminate rust marks, try lighter fluid, then cleaning fluid should do the trick. A streaky stainless sink will react well to olive oil on a cloth. Water marks, if they bother you, will come out with rubbing.

If you're concerned about your drain and the pipes it connects to (and I will never forget the night of a dinner party—water backing up in the sink and having to run down the hall to the john to empty this billious-looking pot of filth), once more the warning about grease. Once a week you can give the pipes some Drāno to satisfy their appetite, or, if you don't approve of Drāno, don't want to spend the money or whatever, a half-cup of salt, rinsed down with very hot water, will do a good job, too.

Garbage Disposals

In case you lost the booklet, you should know that they do take care of pretty much everything that comes their way, but they seem to want a tribute from time to time, like a virile young fork or a virgin spoon. If you have a disposal, it won't be news to you that if you have a septic tank as well your septic tank is going to fill about twice as fast. When you push your three pounds plus of garbage a day down that little pathway, you might begin to wonder whether there is a better way to deal with it. If you have room for a septic tank, you should have room for a compost heap where you put all those lovely vegetable peels and melon skins. Then you put the compost on your potted plants and your vegetable garden or rose bushes and you will grow gorgeous things. Recycle. Recycle.

Don't use Drāno if you have a disposal. Keep after the food on its way down with a strong flow of cold water. Toss a lemon down from time to time, or a grapefruit or an orange—it will make it smell nice. And getting back to that old septic tank, don't use your disposal to dispose of egg shells, grounds, and bones. If you must throw fats down, make sure they're well flushed with plenty of cold water.

The Dishwasher

I must admit that before I had a dishwasher I used to go around telling anyone who listened to me that I really couldn't see the sense of it, it seemed to take just as long. What I know now that I didn't know then was that the beauty of it is that you have all that wonderful space. The important thing to know about your dishwasher is how many washes it provides. The easiest way to find this out is by looking in your instruction manual, but you probably have misplaced it, so look in the dishwasher: if it has two cups, one of which is covered, it probably washes the dishes twice, in which case you're lucky. If your dishwasher provides two washing cycles merely:

Put in your dishes.

Put in your soap, and let 'er go.

If, on the other hand, you have to struggle by one just one soap cup or none at all (you put 2 tablespoons dishwasher stuff in the bottom of the machine) you will have to follow this ritual:

1. Scrape the dishes.
2. Get the egg off, loosen it with salt if you need to.
3. Wipe off any grease.

In either case, whether you're one-cup or two-cup, you should remember to put silver in with the handles down to minimize spotting. And the following things should not by rights be machine washed.

1. Antique china
2. Iron skillets (the long immersion ruins their oiled finish)
3. Dishes with gold and silver bands (they'll fade, but not all that much)
4. Sharp knives (the rubbing up against neighbors dulls their edge)
5. Soft plastic (it will melt and get out of shape)
6. Rubber of any kind
7. Long-stemmed goblets that are delicate

If you're willing to spend the extra time and expense, a one-wash cycle machine can become a two-wash cycle machine by the simple expedient of resetting it at the end of its wash cycle and adding more detergent. Or you can put dishes through a rinse cycle after every meal, turning it on after the final loading. Problems with dishwasher and washed dishes:

1. There is crud all over my glasses
   a. You're probably not scraping well enough.
   b. Check the trap at the bottom, if there is one. It traps food particles and may be sending them right back up at your stuff.
   c. You may be letting things sit in there too long.
   d. You may be misloading. Check instructions, and avoid heavy pots.
2. There's a hazy film over all my dishes and glasses
   a. You're probably suffering from an overload of soap and residue left in the machine.
   b. Fix it this way:
      1) Load dishwasher with china and glass only, no silverware.
      2) Put bowl in bottom.
      3) Pour one cup bleach into bowl.
      4) Run through wash and rinse cycle, don't dry.

   5) Fill the bowl with vinegar, go through the
      whole cycle.
This method should remove the film from your glasses
and dishes and also from the inside of the dishwasher
itself, where it's been building. It's a good idea, in any
case, to run your dishwasher through without anything
it in about once a month to clean it out.
   3. My glasses have white spots all over
      a. You can avoid this by pulling them out before
         the drying cycle begins, at the very end of the
         rinse.

How to Wash Dishes

For those of you still struggling with dishpan hands
while your sisters with dishwashers are raising their
I.Q. twenty points a year at the college course they're
attending with all the time saved from doing dishes,
you can get out of the house a little faster if you:
   1. Soak pots, wash out any bowls not previously
      washed.
   2. Fill sink with detergent and very hot water.
   3. Put silver in first; dishes on top; fit the glasses
      on the side.
   4. Let water get cold; then drain out water.
   5. Swish dishes under hot water faucet, rubbing off
      remaining crud with sponge or dishcloth.
   6. Stack the dishes in a dish drainer rack (a separate
      glass rack is helpful if you have room). The
      silverware should be put handles up for less spot-
      ting.
   7. If you have a sprayer thing at your sink, turn the
      water to very hot and spray the dishes on the
      drainboard. This should cause the dishes to dry
      without spots, although the silverware should be
      wiped if you care about spots.

SPECIAL PROBLEMS

If somebody gets lipstick on your china cups or glasses, bleach will take it off without rubbing.

If there's a brown icky film on the jar of water you keep in your refrigerator, shake it up with some warm water, a tablespoon full each of rice, baking soda, and vinegar, rinse and let dry.

To clean an eggbeater, beat it in soap suds. If you've let the egg congeal, you've probably got to take it off with steel wool and salt.

For pots with egg sticking to them, soak in cold water; for plates with egg, rinse in cold water—hot water sets the egg more.

To clean a grinder that you've been grinding things in, grind a piece of bread through it.

To clean a blender, empty it out, squeeze in some mild detergent and fill it about one third full of warm water. Then turn it on and let it run a while.

If you have a narrow-neck bottle or vase, and you don't have a bottle brush or can't get it in, put in some raw rice or crushed eggshells, some detergent, vinegar, and warm water and shake it.

If there are stains in your teapot or coffeepot, soak them overnight in warm water and a tablespoon of dishwasher compound.

You can get the rust off rusty knives by sticking them in an onion for a half an hour, washing them, and polishing them.

If you have a scorched pan, soak it overnight in bleach, diluted about four to one.

Barbecue skewers clean easily if stuck through a steel wool soap pad.

Don't use steel wool or sink cleanser on plastic dinnerware. If there are stains in the cup, soak in baking soda and water.

If the grounds won't come out of your coffeemaker

basket, sit it in a warm oven for fifteen minutes or so. The heat will dry the grounds so they can be shaken out.

You probably know that you don't use steel wool or an abrasive cleaner on Teflon or coated pots and pans. If something gets hopelessly stuck to it, put in one cup water, 1 cup bleach, two tablespoons baking soda, and boil it for ten minutes. Wash it and dry it and rub it with salad oil and reseason it.

If your iron skillet is really grungy looking and coated with grease, using it on an outside grill will help burn off the old grease.

If your cast-iron skillet is rusty, wash it in soap and hot water, using steel wool if necessary. If that doesn't work, put some kerosene on the steel wool. Then coat it inside and out with vegetable oil. Letting the skillet sit out wet is what got it rusty in the first place.

If you have discolored aluminum, fill a large pot, preferably aluminum, with hot water, and after it's boiling throw in two tablespoons cream of tartar. Boil it for about half an hour, then go over it with a steel wool soap pad and soap.

If something of stainless steel is too dirty to clean with soap and water, try warm water and ammonia.

If two glasses stick together you can get them apart by putting them in a bowl of hot water and filling the upper one with cold water. (Cold contracts and heat expands, in case you didn't know.)

Tin that has to be cleaned should be cleaned gently; it's a thin coat over iron and if rubbed too hard will go through to the iron. So use fine steel wool, if you have to rub.

If your breadbox is rusty, sand off the rust with sandpaper then wipe it with a damp cloth and dry it thoroughly.

If you have anything that's enamel, bleach will take out the stains. If there's food stuck to it, boil it with cream of tartar.

Brown stain on stainless steel will come off with Brillo and cleanser.

I strongly suggest not buying copper-bottom pots since they're yet another source of guilt and work. However, if you do have them, don't hang them on a pegboard where they'll be displayed; keep them in the stove where no one will ever see their dirty bottoms.

When polishing silver, try to use long strokes, rather than circular ones. This will make a somewhat prettier patina. Paste polishes have the advantage that you can stick the fork tines down in them for about five minutes and you won't have to be a contortionist to get the insides of the tines clean. Liquid polishes do, however, tend to cut tarnish faster. If you don't have a silver chest, at least keep your silver in a drawer with some Pacific cloth. They'll tarnish less quickly. Use a brush for polishing filigree, a toothbrush is a little bit too hard, but a soft old one is okay.

There is a process called electrolytic polishing that removes tarnish. However, it does such a uniformly good job that there's no shading left in figured pieces and the stuff tends to come out looking more like stainless than silver. However, you might try it on one piece someday, and if you like it it's certainly easier.

Boil up a quart of water, add 1 tablespoon baking soda and 1 tablespoon ordinary salt in an aluminum pan. If it's not aluminum, crinkle up some Reynolds Wrap and throw it in. Put the silver in and boil four or five minutes.

Don't put in anything that has glue or felt, like candlesticks.

By the way, both salt and rubber are harmful to sterling. So don't ever tie it up with a rubber band, because it will leave an impossible stain. And rinse out silver salt cellars or the salt will corrode them.

A few last things before we leave the kitchen:

About Knives: If you're in the market for utility knives, buy ones with serrated edges; they almost always seem to cut and never need sharpening. It makes sense to have a knife rack for two reasons: it keeps your knives from knocking around together and losing their sharp edges and it keeps you or anyone else from getting a cut when you stick a hand in the drawer. Never put a knife in a flame and use a can opener, not a knife, to pry off lids and things like that.

Fires: Some year for Christmas, Georg Jensen will come out with a teak and platinum fire extinguisher at which point loads of people will receive it as a present. Because, somehow, nobody ever has a fire extinguisher in an apartment and not too many homeowners have them either. Besides telling you that you should buy yourself a fire extinguisher right before you call up the dentist, I could tell you a few elementary things about kitchen fires:

1. Most of the fires in the kitchen are grease fires— fat catching fire. Grease is a kind of oil and, as you know, oil and water don't mix. So, if you throw water onto the grease, water, being heavier, will sink, often causing the burning grease to overflow and spread—so NO WATER on grease fires. If a fire does start, use:

2. Baking soda or, in a pinch, salt. Baking soda releases carbon dioxide, which is good, and salt smothers the fire, which is good. If you use salt in an oven fire, get it out afterwards, using a pancake turner.

3. If something like a steak catches fire under the broiler, you may quickly wet a dishcloth, ring it out and throw it over. This will smother the flames and the steak will still be edible.

4. A fire in a pot can usually be put out by clamping the lid on, which smothers the flames by cutting out access to oxygen.

5. A fire in the wastebasket probably was caused by

a lighted match or cigarette and for this sort of
fire you may use WATER.

6. If you're out of baking soda, never try to put out
a grease fire with cornstarch or flour. The small
particles ignite and you're out of the frying pan,
and out of the fire, as it were, into something
rather unpleasant.

Smells

If you're stuck with a bad smell in your kitchen and
you don't have a deodorizer spray, you can:

1. Fill a saucer full of vinegar which will not make
the room smell of vinegar, but rather will neutralize things.
2. Cut up an onion and put it in a dish which will,
it is true, make the room smell of onions but it
may be better than what it smells of.
3. Burn a tablespoon of coffee (fresh) on a stove
burner.

Now there are a great many other things in the house
that need cleaning from time to time. Many things, like
lamps and lampshades, picture frames, andirons, fireplaces, old antique pewter loving cups, and the like
don't really need cleaning from year to year as long as
the dust is kept from adhering to them and turning to
dirt. Say, however, for the sake of argument that you
think you might want to give everything a going over
about once a year (hopefully rotating it). What follows,
then, is a guide to clean just about everything that
wasn't covered before. And some tips on how to care
for:

BEDSTEADS

If they're very old wood, wipe them with a rag wrung
out in citronella, or so they say. If they're enameled
metal beds, wipe with soap and water. If there are

spots, rub very gently with a sponge and small amount of sink cleanser. If they're brass beds, wipe them off with a dry dusting cloth, then rub with lemon oil.

CANDLES

If you run across a pair of white candles that are perfectly all right except that they're dusty, you can clean them with denatured alcohol on a rag. By the way, there are probably fifty ways to keep candles from tipping over, but the best one I've found is to use a non-hardening child's modeling clay like Gloppy. If you have no Gloppy at your house, use clay. Melting the bottom of a candle with a match will also work most of the time if the fit isn't too far off.

CHROME OR STAINLESS STEEL

A detergent solution or glass spray cleaner put on with a rag and rubbed off with a soft dry rag will do it.

COPPER AND BRASS

Either use a standard copper or brass cleaner, or, if you want a less shiny surface, mix some linseed oil and pumice powder. A little lemon oil from time to time on the old andirons wouldn't hurt.

ENAMEL

Rust spots in a tub: Fill the tub with hot water. Add 1 cup bleach. Let it stand overnight. Keep the rubber mats in. They'll get whiter, too.

ENAMEL FAUCETS

If you have enamel faucets and you've always wondered how to get them clean, rub them with a soft rag dipped in ammonia. Wash them with hot water and soap. Polish with a soft dry cloth.

FIREPLACES

Tile fireplaces can be cleaned once a year by applying salt on a raw lemon (yummy) and rubbing, then scrubbing with soap and water. If you coated a brick fireplace with a thin coat of liquid wax, it wouldn't get as smoked up.

GLASS

Use Windex or glass wax to clean it and polish it off with a clean dry cloth or a chamois. Virtually nothing other than breaking it can harm it, but if your young kids use your glass coffee table for a coloring book, just rub the crayon off with a dry rag, preferably smooth cotton.

IVORY

If it's too yellow for your taste, wet it with denatured alcohol and let it sit in the sunlight. If it is just dirt, wipe off with a rag dampened in denatured alcohol.

HOUSE PLANTS

It should be noted that I have what is commonly referred to as a black thumb. At a glance from me your usual hardy house plant withers and dies. However, I am fortunate in having a husband whose way with plants is exceeded only by his way with people (hear, hear!). He passes along the following hints:

1. Find out when you buy what plant is best suited to the conditions you expect to subject it to—sun, shade, a dry room, or whatever.

2. Plants thrive best when the atmosphere is not too dry—so use a humidifier in winter if you really care. You can spray the leaves with an atomizer once a week (or a flit gun, but don't leave water in it or it will rust through).

3. Overwatering kills more plants than underwatering. Twice a week is plenty for most plants. When in doubt, don't.

4. A glazed container is better than a clay pot—because it isn't as porous, so the soil doesn't dry out as quickly. Make sure that any pot into which you put a plant has drainage.

5. Watering with lukewarm water is good.

6. If you cut off a brown spot, leave about ½ inch between brown and green or else it will bruise and brown more.

7. You can brighten leaves with mineral oil, dabbed on with cotton.

8. You can save a little money on your initial plant purchase if what you want is a tall plant peeking out from behind something. If its base isn't within view, just set it up on another pot that's inverted, or a stack of books, or what you will.

9. If you turn your plant from time to time all parts will get their ration of life-giving sunlight.

LAMPSHADES

Take the cellophane cover off a lampshade as soon as you get it home, or else it will streak and yellow. If a lampshade is slightly soiled, you can probably get the stain out by rubbing lightly with cheesecloth that has been dipped in cleaning fluid. Use an old shaving brush to clean a pleated shade.

LEATHER
Clean it with saddle soap (see the saddle soap container). Buff it with a chamois.

MARBLE
If the surface is dull, buff it with a hand polisher if you happen to have one. If it's stained, well, that's what marble stain remover at your local hardware store is for.

PEWTER
Treat it like silver (which we left somewhere in the kitchen).

PLASTIC
Use soap and water or a spray cleaner. Don't use an abrasive cleaner. Rub crayon off as with glass.

PIANOS
A piano should ideally be tuned three times a year—but don't have it tuned for three months after you move—the wood has to have a chance to settle. Don't place it near extremes of heat and cold—it doesn't belong near a fireplace, window, radiator, or register. Don't close the keyboard off from sunlight constantly—the keys will turn yellow. If you need to clean the keys, put some denatured alcohol on a soft cloth and rub gently. Wring out the cloth well. If the keys are yellowed, you can keep them wet with denatured alcohol for a while and let them dry in the sunlight. Polish with a chamois.

PICTURE FRAMES

When the time comes to clean the glass on the picture frames, spray the liquid onto a cloth and apply it to the glass, because if it gets into the joints it might weaken the glue or damage the finish. If you have gilt picture frames, moisten a sponge with a solution of half ammonia and half denatured alcohol and pat the frame gently. Pat it dry and put on a little lemon oil with a piece of cheesecloth.

RADIATORS AND REGISTERS

If you've been keeping the dust off them, you should maybe twice a year get behind the radiator with a brush and get it clean back there. Give registers a thorough vacuuming every few months, in addition to their cursory regular one.

RECORDS

If they get a lot of glop on them, you can wash them. Actually, I suggest you practice on a ratty old record first, and if it works for you, you can go on to your limited-pressing Carusos.

Fill the kitchen sink with a weak solution of Ivory Soap or Joy and water. Dip the record into the solution and wipe with a soft cloth in the direction of the grooves. Rinse under lukewarm water, using a sponge. Avoid getting the label wet. Let dry without wiping. This should remove fingermarks, dust, and grease.

WROUGHT IRON

You should get the dust off with a damp cloth. If it's become rusty, scouring with steel wool and a liquid rust remover should do it.

Well, I suppose it's conceivable that you have something in your house that's not made of any of the above, or of any of the things we've been over before. But if you've grasped the chemical principles of cleaning:

1. Don't let a porous surface get very wet or it will change in some way.
2. Don't use a scratchy cleaner on something smooth.
3. Begin with the mildest cleaning agent and work up from there.

You should be able to extrapolate pretty well.

I have tried, really really tried, to be organized about this. I mean, I wanted to avoid one of those roundup chapters that just seem to meander on with no unifying force. (I am, as you may have noticed, very big on unifying forces.) Unfortunately, I find myself with a fairly good number of pretty decent ideas on how to make things easier, all covering situations in which one is likely to find oneself. I therefore descend into miscellany, although I seem to have a rather abundant number of things to say about paint. But everyone paints something sometime.

If you need an emergency glue and you don't have any, colorless nail polish will hold for a while. It's worth a try.

If you have squeaky hinges and they bother you, you can use plain old Vaseline to unsqueak them.

If you should happen to have a door that's warped and doesn't close right and it's an important door and you care, tack some sandpaper on the floor under the door. It will then cure itself in time, and is much easier than taking the door off the hinges and sanding it.

If you're screwing something into wood, stick the screw into a bar of soap and it will go in more easily.

If you're hammering in a nail or a picture hook, if you just put a piece of Scotch tape over where the hole is going to be, the probability factor of cracks is significantly lessened.

It's a good idea to map your fuse box if you have one, since this will save you the bother of trying all the holes to find out which one blew. If your fuse box is in the basement, plug your vacuum cleaner into the dead outlet and, while you're aimlessly changing around fuses, you'll know you've got the right one when you can hear the vacuum cleaner go on.

If you have a battery that's not working, you can try sanding the contact.

If you have ink stains on your finger and it's crucial that you get them off, rub your finger with a wet match. It helps.

If you are down to a totally flat tube of toothpaste and you desperately want to brush your teeth, hold the tube under hot water, then squeeze.

Should you lose a contact lens: Take off your shoes, turn out all the lights except for one bright lamp. Put said bright lamp on the floor and remove the shade. Then look around for a little glittering reflection. You will find fifty pieces of cellophane and, if you're extraordinarily lucky, you might find the lens.

A ballpoint pen that won't write can sometimes be coaxed into a few more lines if you heat the tip with a match. Unless it's plastic and might melt, in which case you should dip it in hot water.

Assuming you need an envelope and all of yours have stuck together in hot weather, put them in the freezer and slide a knife under the flap. This also works for stamps.

You can make your nail polish dry quickly if you stick your hand in the freezer for a few seconds.

Dirty, that is to say smudgy, rubber stamps can be cleaned in hot soapy water.

If you're having a party and need lots of room for ice, you could use your washing machine as an extra ice bucket.

If you have doubts about how reliable your scale is (unfortunately it's usually quite reliable), you can get an idea of its reliability by laying a five- or ten-pound bag of sugar or something that happens to be unopened on it. A half-full bag of sugar will not do the trick.

When you're tying a package, wet the cord first and it will dry taut.

To remove the price from a package, put a piece of Scotch tape over it, rub, and remove. The price should come off with the tape. On the other hand, both the price and the tape might stay on. In which case you're worse off and will have to go out and buy another present if you care that much.

If you happen to be moving, God forbid, one small thing you can do to make it easier is to wrap your dishes in towels instead of in newspaper. Then you won't have to wash them all before you sit down to your meager moving-in dinner.

You might try to remember to stick a plastic bag in your suitcase where it will be handy for wet things or dirty laundry.

If you happen to be the kind of person who sends cookies by mail, packing them in popcorn will keep them from crumbling and will also provide something to eat if your cookies are inedible by the time they arrive.

At the same time that you put the plastic bag in your suitcase, put in a couple of bars of nice smelling soap. So you have the soap that you usually forget, and also your suitcase smells nice.

If you have a cat and have to give him medicine, spill it on his fur and he will be faced with a terrible conflict almost always resolved by licking the stuff off, since he is not a total slob.

This strikes me as very sensible and one of these days I mean to do it. If you put some sand in your car ashtrays, you will not be faced with the unpleasantness of driving for fifty miles while choking to death. If you happen to do that, get some more sand and put it in fifty-pound bags in the trunk of your car where it will be when you need it when it's icy.

If you have trouble pulling into a garage and hit the wall half of the time and wind up with the back end out of the garage the other half of the time, hang a piece of string from the roof of the garage at the point where your windshield will hit it if you've pulled in far enough.

It is said that waxing a snow shovel with paste wax makes snow shoveling easier. I wouldn't know, but it sounds as though it might.

Flies will not be so prone to roost in your garbage if you sprinkle dry soap powder in the bottom. This will work much better if you clean out your garbage cans first, which you won't, but it does help a little.

Ants are supposed to be phobic about chalk lines and won't cross them. Which is good to know. You could draw a line around your sugar bowl, or something like that.

Now then, about painting, about which I seem to know so much:

You can plan ahead to keep yourself clean by—

If you're painting something up high, put on a rubber glove and turn the cuff up and a good part of the paint will wind up in there.

If you slather your face with cold cream, you need only slather it off and paint will come with it.

If you wear glasses, plastic wrap over the lenses will protect them.

For the lot that remains on your face, try baby oil or butter before you resort to turpentine, which is not exactly what Elizabeth Arden recommends in her good skin care program. And if you have the foresight to transfer your turpentine to something like an old Windex bottle, it will last forever and ever and not slop out into the sink.

Put Vaseline or petroleum jelly on hinges if you're

painting doors or cabinets and the paint flecks will come off easily. (The more clever of you will see that this is precisely the same principle as putting cold cream on your face. In fact, there's absolutely no reason why you can't use cold cream for hinges, if you don't have vaseline.)

Should you happen to be painting outside around the windows and you don't like scraping paint off the windows, spray the glass with liquid detergent like Ivory and when the paint dries, turn the garden hose on the windows.

However, splatters on windows can be removed with nail polish remover.

An old eggbeater will stir up paint very nicely. But if you happen to buy your paint long in advance of your project, keep it in the trunk of your car where it will be agitated enough to keep it from congealing.

The simple placement of a common paper plate under the paint can you're using will avoid a lot of mess. If you're interrupted while you're painting, wrapping the brushes in plastic wrap will keep them moist until you return.

When you close up the paint can, paint a strip of paint at the level of the paint. This will enable you to see what color it is and tell how much is left, if you want to use it again, without going through the trial of opening the paint can.

It would be awfully foresighted of you to put a small quantity of leftover paint in little jars. Then when something got marred, you could just swab over the spot with a piece of absorbent cotton dipped in the paint.

And if you can't stand the smell of paint, cutting up an onion and leaving it in the painty place will neutralize the odor.

XII

Twelve Rules for Mental Health

And Then Some

Rules for Mental Health

(Which you may find in *The Household Encyclopedia* by N. H. and S. K. Mager, should you happen to have it.*)

A large proportion of illnesses have been found to be caused by emotional disturbances which seem to have absolutely no relation to the disease itself. Some of us are fortunate enough to be able to control our emotions, others, on the contrary, allow them to run rampant or suppress them unduly.

Here are some hints that may prove helpful in maintaining good mental health.

1. Try not to worry. Time minimizes all troubles. Postpone until tomorrow what you are worrying about today.

2. Don't brood over the past. Think about the rosy future.

3. Make the best of each situation. Nothing is really as bad as it appears at first.

4. Envy is a natural feeling. Try, nevertheless, to

---

* Pocket Books, New York, 1968. $0.95 at this writing.

limit your desires to things which are reasonably obtainable.

5. Cultivate a tolerance for the opinions and emotions of others. Remember that other people have emotions very similar to yours.

6. Cultivate a sense of humor.

7. Find an interesting hobby. Above all, keep busy, and you will find you have no time for emotional upsets.

8. If you have something bothering you, let it out. Keeping it to yourself makes it grow.

9. If something's gone wrong, don't look for a scapegoat to let it out on. Take a walk till you're relaxed.

10. Remember, everybody needs love and appreciation. A few kind extra words or a surprise gift will do wonders.

11. If you have something unpleasant to do, do it immediately and get it over with. Worrying about it will probably bother you more than doing it.

12. Families are important, but remember, every member of the family has a life of his own to lead.

I have considered mimeographing the above rules for my husband to pass out to his patients on their first visit, the way diet doctors give you lists of foods you can eat all you want of (boiled rutabaga, moldy bread toasted without butter, fresh caviar). Or perhaps just one copy in large type that he could paste on the inside of his desk drawer and refer to when he had a difficult case.

There's nothing wrong with these rules. (Notice how they're called rules—not suggestions or ideas, but *Rules*.) It's just that they're totally impossible to follow as well as being completely simplistic. They're dandy for dealing with problems like what color to paint the living room, but they tend to fall apart when the situation is just a tiny bit complex. So I have worked out a far more realistic and probably equally useless guide to mental health which I give you now forthwith.

Rule One: Don't do too much.

Rule Two: Make sure you know where your emergency exit is.

Rule Three: Reality test regularly.

Rule One: Don't Do Too Much

A lot of women get into trouble (actually, so do a lot of men and so do a lot of children, and so do a lot of newts, but one must write about what one knows) when they take on too much. I give you the example of a person I know quite intimately who was managing to keep her head together reasonably well, raising two little children, doing a little writing, and keeping up her house in a relatively civilized level when she:

1. Signed a contract to do a book.
2. Took a job three days a week.
3. Decided to redecorate the apartment.
4. Determined to lose twenty pounds.

The first week was marked by the euphoria characteristic of that first week you're off cigarettes when you know you've got it licked and your strength is as the strength of ten because your lungs are pure. The second week she decided that there was no good reason why the book had to be started right away, considering there were six whole months to write it in. After about two months, she decided it might be time to get to work on the book and let the house go in mid-air, looking somewhat more depressing than it had two months before. Then she started spending whole days at work figuring out color schemes and topics for chapters and budgets for 1972 and eating Nestlé Crunch bars. Finally, five months later and ten pounds heavier than when she had begun, she began working until two in the morning on the book, totally neglecting everything else.

We have here a simple case of overloaded circuits. Generally when the circuits start overloading, the first thing you'll find is that everything is suffering a little bit—kind of a brownout of the functions; then one by one things go completely to hell. So get to know your limitations; if you start to load up all at once with a lot more than you'd previously been taking on, give some thought to what's motivating you. It's a curious thing that a minor loss of functioning rarely results in a cutback of self-demand; more frequently what happens is a tendency to do more, as though a failure in one area—real or imagined—has to be made up in another area. Speaking of failure, you could postulate, if you wanted to, that some people are frightened of success and when it appears within their grasp, they may fight it by making the job too hard to accomplish (or blowing it so out of proportion that they can justify failure by saying, in effect, it's too impossible for anyone to do).

Rule Two: Make Sure You Know Where Your Emergency Exit Is

This doesn't necessarily at all mean find a hobby—although it's not inconceivable that that might do the trick. It means find something that will knit you back together as quickly as possible—either when your emotions are getting nippy or when a situation is major to minor intolerable. Let's say, for the sake of argument, that you've had a morning like the following:

1. The baby woke up at 6:00 A.M. with diarrhea and a shredded Pamper.

2. You forgot that today was the day of the teacher's conference and your six-year-old is home for the day and the television set is broken.

3. The bank called to tell you you were overdrawn for the third time this month.

4. You have discovered a new species of bug nesting in your lower kitchen cabinets.

5. The dress you expected to wear to the cocktail party tonight came back from the cleaner with a little tag that said that the red blotch in back couldn't be removed from the garment without danger to the material.

Which goes to show that it isn't always the big things that drive you crazy and nobody knows the trouble the little things can be. Except I do. Through dint of sheer superhuman effort and the remarkable will to survive through adversity that characterizes the human race, you have managed to get your child over to his grandmother's, your baby is napping, and, although nothing much else is improved, there is nothing that has to be attended to within the next thirty minutes. This is not, by God, the point to take stock. This is a situation that calls for emergency first aid and you should have it at hand. You should have something that will calm you down sufficiently to make it possible to face the rest of the day when the baby wakes up, your child returns, and the water boiler explodes. I have taken a survey of all my friends who are still walking around after what seems like years of days like this and I pass on to you the following methods for getting it all back in one piece again:

1. Falling on the bed with a tuna fish sandwich and a mystery novel.

2. Playing solitaire.

3. Playing solitaire without cheating.

4. Watching a soap opera on TV.

5. Doing twenty sit-ups.

6. Going outside and killing a whole lot of ants on the sidewalk.

7. Calling up mother and crying.

8. Calling up a friend and crying.

9. Getting out a lot of cookbooks and planning superb menus.

10. Making a list of every dress you own and putting next to each dress a list of every accessory you can wear with it.

11. Playing tennis.

12. Cursing a whole lot.

13. Having a drink.

Now all these things are just different ways of repressing or sublimating, or displacing, when you come to think of it. But they are the homely little defense mechanisms we use day to day. All these things have in common the use of a fair number of brain cells in one directed direction, so directed as to make it more difficult to concentrate on the things that are bugging you. In the case of somebody who finds it preferable to eat something—if the crises are frequent—you're probably going to find someone who is not right out there in the forefront of bikini wearers. And someone who decides that drinking is what it takes had better not need the pieces put together three times a day or you've got the not uncommon alcoholic housewife. So while nobody is advocating washing woodwork or closet cleaning, just make sure the escape hatch doesn't get to be more trouble than it's worth.

Rule Three: Reality Test Regularly

When you find yourself doing a whole lot of things you don't usually do—particularly if they follow some moderately major change in your life style, take a long, cold, appraising look at how you're doing, as compared to how you've been doing, or how everybody you know is doing. If you don't like what you see, start dropping pressures one by one, if you possibly can, because your defenses are overloading and you need all the symptomatic relief you can get. If you'll remember all that stuff about checks and balances we talked about in Chapter II.

As for me, I have twelve people coming for dinner, my daughter has just smeared peanut butter on the living room couch, I am afraid to pick up the phone because there is this magazine editor who is going to kill me because I am five weeks late with an article, and I am off to eat a tuna fish sandwich while I sort out all my old buttons according to weight.

The End

BALLANTINE BOOKS BRINGS YOU NOTHING BUT THE BEST IN FICTION